Columbia University

Contributions to Education

Teachers College Series

No. 523

AMS PRESS
NEW YORK

EDUCATIONAL OPPORTUNITIES PROVIDED FOR POSTGRADUATE STUDENTS IN PUBLIC HIGH SCHOOLS

BY

EINAR W. JACOBSEN, Ph.D.

TEACHERS COLLEGE, COLUMBIA UNIVERSITY

CONTRIBUTIONS TO EDUCATION, NO. 523

Published with the Approval of
Professor Grayson N. Kefauver, Sponsor

BUREAU OF PUBLICATIONS
Teachers College, Columbia University
NEW YORK CITY
1932

Library of Congress Cataloging in Publication Data

Jacobsen, Einar William, 1893–
  Educational opportunities provided for postgraduate
students in public high schools.

  Reprint of the 1932 ed., issued in series: Teachers
College, Columbia University. Contributions to
education, no. 523.
  Originally presented as the author's thesis, Columbia.
Includes bibliographical references.
  1. High schools—United States—Postgraduate work.
I. Title. II. Series: Columbia University. Teachers
College. Contributions to education, no. 523.
LB1695.J3 1972   374.8   73-176905
ISBN 0-404-55523-3

Reprinted by Special Arrangement with Teachers
College Press, New York, New York

From the edition of 1932, New York
First AMS edition published in 1972
Manufactured in the United States

AMS PRESS, INC.
NEW YORK, N. Y.   10003

ACKNOWLEDGMENTS

The writer is indebted to Professor Grayson N. Kefauver for the direction and guidance given to this study and to Professor Carter Alexander and Professor Thomas H. Briggs for their critical and constructive suggestions. He is grateful to the high school principals who coöperated by making the data available, and to Gladys Garner Jacobsen, who by her encouragement, help, and coöperation made this study possible.

E. W. J.

CONTENTS

v

EDUCATIONAL OPPORTUNITIES PROVIDED FOR POSTGRADUATE STUDENTS IN PUBLIC HIGH SCHOOLS

CHAPTER I

THE POSTGRADUATE PROBLEM IN PUBLIC HIGH SCHOOLS

STATEMENT OF THE PROBLEM

The knowledge that the average worker in the secondary school field possesses about postgraduate students is usually limited to the personal experiences he or his fellow teachers may have had with this type of student. As a result of these contacts, he may be convinced that the high school graduate who returns for additional work is a troublesome disturber of the good order of the school, and therefore should not be encouraged to return. There are others who are of the opinion that these students are serious minded and deserving of help and consideration.

With the increase in the number of postgraduates in the public high schools of the United States, many principals and teachers are seeking for facts which may be of help to them in arranging an intelligent program for these students instead of depending upon their own limited experience. There is nothing in professional literature in the secondary field which can give the facts about the 29,225 postgraduates in the United States. Their distribution is indicated in Table I.

This first study of the postgraduate problem in our public high schools is intended to explore the field sufficiently to bring out such facts concerning the educational opportunities now provided for postgraduate students, as well as such traits or characteristics which may be possessed by these students as a group, as will be helpful to the secondary school principal or teacher confronted with this problem.

TABLE I

Undergraduate and Postgraduate High School Enrollment for Each State in the United States for 1929-1930

State	High School Enrollment	Number of Postgraduates
Alabama	106,106	79*
Arizona	13,592*	294*
Arkansas	40,535	22*
California	276,418	3,371
Colorado	36,095	136
Connecticut	52,397	281
Delaware	7,009	14*
District of Columbia	15,170	126
Florida	44,148	97*
Georgia	50,023	0
Idaho	21,000	47
Illinois	286,635	8,28ɔ*
Indiana	130,000	135
Iowa	124,389	192
Kansas	108,353	330
Kentucky	59,331	25
Louisiana	51,000	0
Maine	33,648	142*
Maryland	47,614*	0
Massachusetts	147,618	1,276*
Michigan	188,233	1,503*
Minnesota	112,625*	750*
Mississippi	28,428*	13
Missouri	120,000	194*
Montana	26,694	307
Nebraska	70,395	103
Nevada	3,628	56
New Hampshire	20,803	438
New Jersey	126,877	354
New Mexico	10,995	61
New York	491,696	7,424
North Carolina	125,000	266
North Dakota	21,540*	21*
Ohio	333,935	200
Oklahoma	104,000	126
Oregon	49,065	192*
Pennsylvania	660,455	595
Rhode Island	21,576	155*
South Carolina	40,020	22
South Dakota	26,088	98
Tennessee	56,660	81
Texas	250,000	175
Utah	33,452	13
Vermont	13,200	67
Virginia	79,081	40
Washington	85,428	500
West Virginia	51,802*	241*
Wisconsin	118,251	150
Wyoming	11,164	233
Total	**4,932,172**	**29,225**

* United States Bureau of Education *Bulletin* No. 35 for 1927-1928. Department of Interior, Washington, D. C.

DEFINITION OF THE TERM POSTGRADUATE

For the purposes of this study a postgraduate student is defined as one who returns for additional school work after having been officially graduated from a public high school.

THE NATURE OF THE INVESTIGATION

The first question considered in this study was the determination of the extent of the postgraduate problem in the United States. The facts were secured by means of check lists sent to the State Superintendents of Public Instruction, and from information received from the Office of Education of the Department of Interior of the Federal Government. Further facts were secured by an examination of the school laws and codes of the various states.

To determine the educational opportunities provided for postgraduate students in public high schools, check lists were sent to a random sampling of schools in all the states reported as having this type of student. Information from five hundred twenty-five schools is included in this study.

For information concerning the traits and characteristics of postgraduate students, check lists were sent to one thousand students of this classification in fifty-five schools selected from the above group. The check lists were filled out under the direction of the local administrators.

Further information was received from secretaries of regional accrediting associations as well as from the secretaries or registrars of the sixty-two leading colleges and universities of the country.

After due consideration of the aspects of the postgraduate problem, the size of the enrollment presented itself to the writer as one aspect to be considered.

HIGH SCHOOL POSTGRADUATE ENROLLMENT

There were 29,225 postgraduates (see Table II) in the public high schools of the United States during the year 1929-1930. This postgraduate enrollment has increased two hundred sixty-six per cent since 1919-1920. The high school enrollment has increased one hundred forty-six per cent for the same period, or less than one-half as much.

An examination of Table I, which shows the postgraduate enrollment in the different states for the year 1929-1930, reveals the fact that the states which have the largest high school enrollment do not always have the largest number of postgraduates; nor does it follow that those which have the smallest high school enrollment have the smallest postgraduate enrollment. The states, in order, having the largest high school enrollment, are: Pennsylvania, first; New York, second; Ohio, third; Illinois, fourth; California, fifth. When the postgraduate enrollment is examined, it is found that Illinois comes first; New York, second; California, third; Michigan, fourth; and Massachusetts, fifth. The states having the smallest postgraduate enrollment are Georgia and Maryland with no postgraduate students, Mississippi and Utah each with thirteen students, and Delaware with fourteen. Further relationships between these states will be brought out later.

The Office of Education of the Department of Interior first included postgraduates in their statistics on public high schools in the year 1919-1920. Postgraduates in the public high schools previous to this date were not enumerated separately. A statement from that office indicates that this classification was included so that their tables would be more accurate.

From Table II it will be seen that there has been an irregular increase, with the exception of one loss, in the postgraduate enrollment in the last ten years. This information was secured from State Superintendents of Public Instruction and from the bulletins of the Office of Education. In 1921-1922 there was a thirteen per cent gain over the period 1919-1920. In the next period, 1923-1924, there was a six per cent decrease. In the year 1925-1926 there was a marked gain of one hundred three per cent in the number of postgraduates. In the following report period there was a small gain of eight per cent and in 1929-1930, a gain of fifty-five per cent. Reports from high school principals indicate a similar increase for the year 1930-1931.

The increase of 1929-1930 is attributed largely to the economic depression. As noted in the next chapter, high school principals reported that a large number of their postgraduate students came back to keep busy until they could secure employment, either permanent or temporary. However, another reason must be

TABLE II

Growth of Postgraduate Enrollment in Public High Schools of the
United States from 1919 to 1930

Year	Postgrad- uate En- rollment	Gain or Loss	Percentage of Gain or Loss Over Previous Report	High School Enrollment
1919–20	7,986*			1,999,106*
1921–22	9,101*	1,115 gain	13% gain	2,496,234*
1923–24	8,492*	609 loss	6% loss	2,950,408*
1925–26	17,319*	8,827 gain	103% gain	3,741,073*
1927–28	18,783*	1,464 gain	8% gain	4,217,313*
1929–30	29,225†	10,442 gain	55% gain	4,932,172†

* Information from United States Bureau of Education *Bulletins* for 1919–1920, No. 37 (1922), for 1921–1922, No. 7 (1924), for 1925–1926, No. 33 (1927), for 1923–1924, No. 40 (1925), and for 1927–1928, No. 35 (1929). Department of Interior, Washington, D. C.

† Based on information received from State Superintendents of Instruction and the Office of Education.

considered in the increase in the number of postgraduates. The so-called tightening up of college requirements often makes it necessary for students to return to high school for additional points or to raise their marks for college entrance. These students enroll as postgraduates. The popularization of education beyond the high school level accounts for a large number of high school graduates returning for additional work. The postgraduate enrollment on the whole, therefore, has increased very definitely during the last ten years, with present indications that the number will be still larger in the future. In some communities serious consideration is being given to the possibility of establishing systematic work beyond the twelfth grade.

DISTRIBUTION OF POSTGRADUATES BY GEOGRAPHICAL AREAS

In order to get a better picture of the distribution of postgraduates in the United States, it is desirable to group the states according to geographical areas. Although the North Central States [1] were in second place in 1919-1920 in postgraduate enrollment, by 1921-1922 they were in first place and have kept that position ever since. The Middle Atlantic States [2] followed along

[1] Ohio, Indiana, Illinois, Michigan, Wisconsin, Minnesota, Iowa, Missouri, Nebraska, Kansas, North Dakota, South Dakota.
[2] New York, New Jersey, Pennsylvania.

in third place in postgraduate enrollment until in 1924 they went up to second place and have continued to occupy that position. The Pacific States [3] started in first place in 1920, then dropped to second in 1923-1924, and since 1925-1926 have occupied the third place in enrollment. The New England States [4] have had a very slow and gradual increase. They started out in fourth place in 1919-1920, and in 1929-1930 were still in the same position. The South Central States,[5] the Plateau States,[6] and the South Atlantic States [7] have had little or no increase in the postgraduate enrollment in the period 1919-1920 to the period 1929-1930.

Table III shows that there has been an increase of 10,442 postgraduates enrolled in 1929-1930 over the number enrolled

TABLE III

COMPARISON OF POSTGRADUATE ENROLLMENT IN DIFFERENT GEOGRAPHICAL SECTIONS OF THE COUNTRY IN 1927–1928 AND IN 1929–1930

SECTION	1927–1928 POSTGRADUATE ENROLLMENT	1929–1930 POSTGRADUATE ENROLLMENT	GAIN	LOSS
New England	1,919	2,359	440	
Middle Atlantic	4,660	8,373	3,713	
South Central	735	521		214
South Atlantic	733	806	73	
North Central	6,519	11,956	5,437	
Plateau	948	1,147	199	
Pacific	3,269	4,063	794	
Total	18,783	29,225	10,656	214
Entire Country			10,442	

in 1927-1928, a growth of fifty-five per cent. This growth has occurred mainly in the North Central and the Middle Atlantic States, with an appreciable gain in the Pacific States.

POSTGRADUATE WORK OFFERED BY OTHER INSTITUTIONS

The information from five hundred twenty-five schools studied by the writer and described in the next chapter indicates that

[3] Washington, Oregon, California.
[4] Maine, New Hampshire, Massachusetts, Vermont, Rhode Island, Connecticut.
[5] Kentucky, Tennessee, Alabama, Mississippi, Arkansas, Louisiana, Oklahoma, Texas.
[6] Montana, Idaho, Wyoming, Colorado, New Mexico, Arizona, Utah, Nevada.
[7] Delaware, Maryland, District of Columbia, Virginia, West Virginia, North Carolina, South Carolina, Georgia, Florida.

institutions other than the regular public high school are offering educational opportunities for the postgraduate student. Among these are the part-time and continuation schools, the trade schools, and the junior colleges. The part-time and continuation schools referred to in Table IV are intended in many states to handle students who finish the minimum full-time requirements of school but who are still required to have part-time education

TABLE IV

COMPARISON OF POSTGRADUATE ENROLLMENT WITH NUMBER OF HIGH SCHOOLS
REPORTING OTHER INSTITUTIONS PROVIDING EDUCATIONAL
OPPORTUNITIES FOR THESE STUDENTS

NUMBER OF POSTGRADUATES	INSTITUTION				
	Continuation and Part-Time Schools	Trade Schools	Junior Colleges	Other Colleges	Total
65–above	0	0	1	0	1
60–64	0	0	0	1	1
55–59	0	0	0	0	0
50–54	0	0	0	0	0
45–49	0	0	0	0	0
40–44	0	0	0	0	0
35–39	1	1	1	1	4
30–34	0	0	1	1	2
25–29	3	2	0	1	6
20–24	1	0	1	3	5
15–19	1	0	1	2	4
10–14	1	2	2	2	7
5– 9	7	6	9	9	31
0– 4	6	5	14	15	40
Total	20	16	30	35	101

until they have reached a certain age. They also provide educational opportunities for adults in afternoon and evening classes. These schools, in most instances, give short commercial courses. In a few cases college preparatory subjects are given. Sixteen schools reported that there were trade schools in their communities which gave definite training for which postgraduates could enroll. Two schools stated that there were special postgraduate departments associated with higher institutions. Thirty high schools reported that the junior colleges in their communities made provision for handling postgraduate students. The other institutions referred to in the table are small colleges which make special provision for students with deficient matriculation units. It is significant that one hundred one high schools reported that institutions such as continuation and part-time schools, trade schools, junior colleges, and other colleges were offering educational opportunities on a secondary level for the high school graduate. The evening schools may also serve to extend the education of students who have obtained a diploma from a high school. Only day schools were canvassed to furnish material for this study.

The presence of these institutions in a community very materially affects the postgraduate load which the regular high school carries. In Table IV it will be noted that, with one exception, the number of postgraduates in the high schools studied does not exceed thirty-nine in communities where other institutions are present. However, trade schools, junior colleges, and colleges are found in communities having high schools of all sizes. Particularly is this true of the junior colleges.

STUDENTS WHO DELAY GRADUATION

In addition to the students who come back for work after formal high school graduation, there is a group of students who delay formal graduation and return for work even though they may have qualified for graduation. Sixteen per cent of the five hundred twenty-five schools studied reported that they had from one to ninety students in their schools who would come under this classification. In addition to this fact, the information gathered in this study shows that delayed graduation is not restricted to schools of any one size.

A feature of the delayed graduation situation is that students with postgraduate standing may be taking work in the same school. This is brought out in Table V. For example, thirty-two schools with one to four postgraduates had as many as nine students who delayed graduation in the same school. It should also be noted that, as a group, schools with the larger number of postgraduates have more students who delayed graduation.

Although these students are not technically postgraduates and

TABLE V

RELATIONSHIP OF POSTGRADUATE ENROLLMENT TO NUMBER OF HIGH SCHOOLS
REPORTING STUDENTS WHO HAVE DELAYED GRADUATION

NUMBER OF POSTGRADUATES	NUMBER WHO DELAY GRADUATION					
	1–9	10–19	20–29	30–39	40– above	Total
65–above	1	0	0	0	0	1
60–64	0	0	0	0	1	1
55–59	0	0	0	0	0	0
50–54	0	0	0	0	0	0
45–49	0	0	1	0	0	1
40–44	0	0	0	0	0	0
35–39	2	2	0	0	0	4
30–34	2	0	0	0	0	2
25–29	3	0	0	0	1	4
20–24	4	1	1	0	0	6
15–19	4	1	1	0	0	6
10–14	4	4	1	0	0	9
5– 9	9	1	0	0	0	10
0– 4	32	2	2	1	1	38
Total	61	11	6	1	3	82

do not appear as such on the school records, they are for all
practical purposes a part of this problem. If these students were
included, the figures on postgraduate enrollment would be larger
than reported earlier in this chapter.

RELATIONSHIP OF THE SIZE OF SCHOOL TO THE POSTGRADUATE ENROLLMENT

A slight relationship exists between the size of the school and
the number of postgraduates.[8] The smaller schools are necessarily limited in the number of postgraduates they may have. The
maximum postgraduate enrollment for the thirty-three per cent
of schools below five hundred students is twenty-nine, whereas
the maximum postgraduate enrollment for schools with more
than four thousand students is one hundred seventy students.
The schools with enrollments from fifteen hundred to three
thousand have a larger range in the postgraduate enrollment
than the other two groups of schools.

[8] Information gained from comparison of check lists by writer.

THE SPRING POSTGRADUATE ENROLLMENT

Another aspect of the postgraduate problem is the increase of the enrollment every year in the spring, in some of the schools. One hundred four, or twenty per cent of the five hundred twenty-five schools studied, indicated an increased enrollment in the spring. In these schools, there was a mean postgraduate enrollment in the fall of eleven, and in the spring, eighteen, or an increase of approximately sixty-four per cent. These schools ranged in size of enrollment from one hundred to seven thousand five hundred.

The postgraduate population is very unstable. As an example of this, the writer, in his study of the problem, received the postgraduate enrollment in the five hundred twenty-five schools studied, in February. Check lists were sent to postgraduates in fifty-five of these schools in March. In the space of five weeks the enrollments had decreased, varying from two to fifty-six per cent for this group of fifty-five schools. This is explained by the fact that it is not compulsory for the students to remain in school, and many leave to accept positions.

THE SIZE OF THE GRADUATION CLASS AND THE NUMBER OF POSTGRADUATES

As was the case in the size of the school and the postgraduate enrollment, there is little relationship between the size of the graduating class and the postgraduate enrollment, except in extreme cases. Of course, small graduation classes will of necessity contribute a small number of postgraduates. Otherwise, we find in the schools studied that one may have a graduating class of more than five hundred students with only five to nine students returning for postgraduate work, but another school, having one hundred students in the graduating class, may have from sixty to sixty-four students coming back for additional work.

CHAPTER II

PROVISIONS MADE BY PUBLIC HIGH SCHOOLS FOR POSTGRADUATE STUDENTS

THE ATTITUDE OF THE STATES

Although the actual furnishing of secondary education to the young people of our country is in the hands of the local communities, the states have a very marked influence on the educational opportunities provided through their appropriations, laws, and judicial decisions. The state superintendent's office also has direct influence, for it carries out these laws and decisions, distributes the funds, determines the state policies, and administers a supervisory program.

An examination of the laws and school codes of the states, together with information received from the offices of state superintendents, reveals the fact that no state makes any direct provision by law for educational opportunities for postgraduate students. Every state does set up, however, certain age limits between which all girls and boys must attend school unless a certain minimum amount of school work has been completed. The age of fourteen appears most frequently. In addition, certain of the states either make it permissive for a person between certain age limits to attend school, or require the public schools to accept persons between certain age limits.

States having legislation which requires schools to accept students between certain ages are as follows:

Wyoming provides by law that "public schools shall be free and accessible to all children resident therein over six and under twenty-one years of age." [1]

The Vermont law says that "the words 'legal pupil' shall mean every child between the ages of six and eighteen years of age but that a person who has become eighteen years of age shall not be deprived of public school advantages on account of age." [2]

[1] Wyoming School Law, 1923-1927, Chap. VI, Sec. 323, p. 115.
[2] Vermont School Law, 1925, Sec. 1243, p. 36.

Pennsylvania provides that "every child, being a resident of any school district in this commonwealth, between the ages of six and twenty-one years may attend the public schools in his district." [3]

Illinois states that the public schools are "for the accommodation of all over the age of six and under twenty-one years." [4]

Florida provides that "nothing . . . shall be so construed as to prevent or prohibit any school or schools from pursuing or completing other, and additional or advanced work." [5]

Arizona provides that "all children between the ages of six and twenty-one who are residents of this state, must be admitted to the schools of this state." [6]

California provides that "the principal may permit deficiencies in high school recommendations to be removed by partial time enrollment in prescribed high school courses while students are completing junior college work; but no high school work taken for the purpose of removing deficiencies shall be allowed to count toward completion of the requirements for junior college graduation." [7]

The state of Maine also permits children to attend public schools between the ages of five and twenty-one years of age." [8]

The laws of these states thus may be said to be permissive in that children between the ages noted cannot be denied the privilege of attending schools. The other states do not have any such provisions as these.

In the absence of laws, some states and one territory have found it necessary to give rulings or state policies in connection with postgraduate problems presented to them. In one instance, a judicial decision brought up the problem.

The following states and territory have made rulings or stated policies on the attendance of postgraduates at public high schools: Hawaii, Oklahoma, Washington, Montana, Ohio, District of Columbia, Idaho, Kansas, and Maryland. The rulings are as follows:

The territory of Hawaii, through its Board of Commission-

[3] Pennsylvania School Law, 1929, Sec. 1401, p. 96, and also Sec. 1703, p. 125.
[4] Illinois School Law, 1921-1927, Sec. 114, Part 9, p. 43.
[5] Florida School Law, 1921-1927, Sec. 1, Chap. 7910, p. 60.
[6] Arizona School Law, 1928, Art. V, Sec. 1033, p. 12.
[7] California School Law, 1929, Sec. 12, Group 2, p. 400.
[8] Communicated to the writer, November 1930.

ers, has made the following rule: "Length of School Attendance. —Except in special cases no student will be permitted to attend senior high school (tenth, eleventh, and twelfth years) more than three years. In case a student is permitted to return to the senior high school for an additional year or fraction of a year beyond the twelfth, it must be clearly seen by the principal that such additional work has definite and sufficient value to the student to warrant such attendance." [9]

The state of Oklahoma has a judicial decision dated April 6, 1928, which refers directly to postgraduate students under a case involving transfer of students. The decision is: "We are unable to find any statute or decision which prohibits the transfer of children of school age from one district to another district where the children have completed a high school course and desire to take a postgraduate course." [10]

The state of Washington takes note of postgraduates by having the following policy in the apportionment of funds: "Attendance is now allowed for state and county funds so long as they take regular high school work. If advanced courses are introduced, they are classified as junior college students and no apportionment is allowed." [11]

The educational officials of Montana have adopted the following policy in reference to postgraduates: "Postgraduates under twenty-one years of age are eligible to attend high school and are included in determining the distribution of funds." [12]

Ohio has adopted the following rule concerning postgraduates: "Admittance is optional with board of education. Tuitional charges are also optional." [13]

The Superintendent of Schools in Washington, D. C., has the following ruling: "Postgraduates must take course of sufficient number of subjects to justify their being bona fide members of school." [14]

The Commissioner of Education for Idaho has ruled as follows: "Tuition pupils do not get tuition the fifth or sixth year." [15]

The State Superintendent of Kansas has ruled that "the priv-

[9] Communicated to the writer, December 6, 1930.
[10] Oklahoma School Law, 1925-1929, Art. II, Sec. 203, p. 57.
[11] Communicated to the writer, November 1930.
[12] *Ibid.*
[13] *Ibid.*
[14] *Ibid.*
[15] *Ibid.*

ileges of public schools are open to all persons between the ages of five to twenty-one years of age whether they be graduated from high school or not." [16]   State Superintendent George A. Allen, Jr., of Kansas, made the following brief comment: "Attempts have been made to refuse admission to pupils who have graduated from high school on their application for additional instruction. We believe this is not in harmony with the true public school spirit."

For the state of Maryland, Superintendent Cook comments: "At the present stage of development of the high school system in Maryland, the State Department of Education does not encourage postgraduate study in the high schools. In fact, I doubt very much if we would consider it a part of the minimum program in the Equalization Fund Counties, if any considerable number of postgraduates were enrolled." [17]

In these states and the one territory there are four concerning themselves with the apportionment of funds. Washington and Montana rule that funds will be available for bona fide postgraduate students, but Idaho and Maryland indicate that funds will not be available for students of this class. In Hawaii it is a question of limiting the attendance. In Oklahoma it is a matter of a high school graduate in one district being given the right to take postgraduate work in another high school district. Kansas and the District of Columbia indicate that the privilege of getting further education is open to postgraduate students, and Ohio leaves it up to the local school board. They may or may not charge tuition of postgraduates as they see fit.

In addition to giving definite information on total high school and postgraduate enrollment, and the laws and rulings for postgraduates, the state officers filling out the check lists were requested to indicate appropriate conditions under which, in their judgment, students should be encouraged to take postgraduate high school work. The reasons upon which judgment was asked were: For the student to earn additional points for college entrance, to make up deficiencies for college entrance, to receive specific vocational training, to keep occupied during unemployment, and to have a definite occupation until old enough to

[16] Communicated to the writer, November 1930.
[17] *Ibid.*

TABLE VI

ATTITUDE OF STATE OFFICERS IN REGARD TO REASONS FOR ENCOURAGING POST-
GRADUATES TO RETURN TO HIGH SCHOOL

REASON FOR ENCOURAGING STUDENTS TO RETURN	NUMBER OF STATE OFFICERS VOTING	
	Yes	No
To earn additional points for college entrance	20	9
To make up deficiencies for college entrance	30	3
To receive specific vocational training	33	3
For occupation during unemployment	20	10
For occupation until old enough to enter college	20	10

enter college. The reasons upon which judgments were asked are
noted in Table VI. A few of the officers did not give an opinion
on any of these reasons, and others checked only a few. Most
of the officers agreed that postgraduates should be encouraged
to return to high school to receive specific vocational training
and to make up deficiencies for college entrance. The agreement
was not so great for other reasons, but at least two-thirds of
those reporting felt that postgraduate students should be encouraged to return for the reasons indicated. The state officers of
three states checked "no" for all the reasons. However, we may
say that the state officers of education in at least twenty states
are not hostile to postgraduates returning for the reasons mentioned above.

The state officers were asked to indicate whether or not they
felt that the colleges and universities in their respective states
should give advanced credit for postgraduate work taken in high
school. Thirty-six officers expressed their judgment on this point.
Seventeen indicated that advanced credit should be given, but
nineteen felt that it should not be given. It is significant that
the official educational representative of as many as seventeen
states should express a favorable attitude.

Some of the states maintain and operate schools on a secondary
level apart from the community high school, such as agricultural
or other specialized schools. There are five hundred sixty-five
institutions in California giving education on a secondary level.
Three of these are special state schools. This represents the
situation in the other states. These schools have not been
included in this study.

NATURE OF INVESTIGATION OF COMMUNITY PROGRAMS

Consideration of the programs sponsored by the local communities should follow a discussion of the states' relation to postgraduate students. The information used in this section was secured from a check list sent to eight hundred schools of all types, selected at random and located in states in which the Office of Education of the Department of Interior reported that postgraduates were enrolled and by information received from State Superintendents of Public Instruction [18] as described in Chapter I. The states having the largest number of postgraduates received the largest number of check lists. A unit of twenty-three was arbitrarily selected. For every twenty-three postgraduate students in a state a check list was sent to a school selected at random in that state. In addition, one hundred lists were sent to schools selected at random in states which reported no postgraduate students, and to schools in large cities having two high schools or more, or types of schools not caught in the first random sampling of eight hundred.

Five hundred twenty-five schools responded in time to be included in this study. This is a fifty-eight per cent return. Out of this number of schools, one hundred ninety-one, or thirty-six per cent, reported no postgraduates for the year 1929-1930, the year for which the information was asked. Many of these schools stated that they had enrolled postgraduates in their schools in previous years, and indicated the policies and regulations in force at that time. These are included in this study. A few of the schools wrote that the reason they did not have postgraduates was that the present economic situation forced the students into employment. In Chapter III, which reports on the postgraduate student, it will be found that this is contrary to the situation in most places. Two schools, recently organized, stated that they did not have postgraduates at present, but they expected to have some in a year or two.

These five hundred twenty-five schools include every size of school. The student enrollment of the schools shown in Table VII ranges from twenty to seven thousand twenty-five, with a median of five hundred ninety-nine and a semi-interquartile range

[18] United States Bureau of Education *Bulletin* No. 35 for 1927-1928. Department of Interior, Washington, D. C.

TABLE VII

DISTRIBUTION OF HIGH SCHOOLS STUDIED ACCORDING TO ENROLLMENT

ENROLLMENT	NUMBER OF SCHOOLS	PERCENTAGE OF TOTAL
5,000–above	5	1.03
4,500–4999	2	.41
4,000–4499	4	.82
3,500–3999	5	1.03
3,000–3499	8	1.66
2,500–2999	12	2.48
2,000–2499	28	5.80
1,500–1999	33	6.84
1,000–1499	56	11.61
500– 999	124	25.72
1– 499	205	42.53
Total	482	99.93

NOTE.—Forty-three schools included in this study did not report their enrollments.

of three hundred forty-two. Forty-two per cent have an enrollment of less than five hundred.

These schools serve the major types of communities. Thirty-five per cent of the schools are serving largely industrial communities; twenty per cent, commercial; seventeen per cent, professional; twenty-seven per cent, agricultural; and less than one per cent are serving other types, such as mining, cattle raising, and fishing. Many of these schools reported that they served mixed communities.

Furthermore, these schools represent the major type of grade organizations found in this country. The largest number of schools reported the nine to twelve grade organization, with the ten to twelve grade organization second, and the seven to twelve organization a close third. The other types referred to in Table VIII include grades nine to thirteen, seven to thirteen, and seven to eleven chiefly. All are accredited either by regional accrediting agencies or by the local state colleges and universities.

The number of postgraduates in these schools is shown in Table IX. The median number of postgraduates is seven, with a range from one to one hundred seventy-nine, with a semi-inter-

TABLE VIII

TYPE OF GRADE ORGANIZATION OF THE SCHOOLS STUDIED

TYPE	NUMBER OF SCHOOLS
10–12	73
6–12	24
7–12	66
9–12	207
8–11	10
8–12	6
9–11	5
Other types	14

NOTE.—One hundred twenty schools included in this study did not report their grade organizations.

quartile range of five. Sixty-one per cent have less than ten postgraduates.

The five hundred twenty-five schools are probably representative of the high schools in the states having postgraduates for these reasons: all sizes of schools are included; they serve the major types of communities; they include the common grade

TABLE IX

DISTRIBUTION OF 334 HIGH SCHOOLS ACCORDING TO NUMBER OF POSTGRADUATES

NUMBER OF POSTGRADUATES	NUMBER OF SCHOOLS	PERCENTAGE OF TOTAL
65–179	9	less than 1%
60–64	2	less than 1%
55–59	2	less than 1%
50–54	2	less than 1%
45–49	1	less than 1%
40–44	7	less than 1%
35–39	8	less than 1%
30–34	6	less than 1%
25–29	8	less than 1%
20–24	19	5%
15–19	21	6%
10–14	44	13%
5– 9	90	26%
1– 4	115	34%

organizations; they have a wide range of the number of post-graduates; and they were selected at random. Some selection may be represented in the failure of forty-two per cent of the schools to respond to the request for information. The nature and extent of selection because of the partial returns cannot be determined. The schools included in the study are representative on the bases which have been noted.

THE ATTITUDE OF HIGH SCHOOLS TOWARD POSTGRADUATES

Before examining the educational opportunities provided for postgraduate students by high schools, one should consider the attitude of these schools toward the graduate who comes back for additional work. In the previous section it was noted that the majority of the official representatives of states expressed an attitude favorable toward high school graduates returning for specific purposes.

As shown by this study of five hundred twenty-five high schools, thirty-three per cent of these schools encouraged post-graduates to return for additional work, eight per cent definitely discouraged these students, and fifty-nine per cent expressed a neutral attitude. The eight per cent of the schools that discouraged postgraduates are located in different parts of the country. Therefore, the discouragement of these students is entirely in the hands of the local school officials. A few of the principals discouraging this type of student volunteered the information that lack of proper facilities for handling these students was responsible for their attitude.

The principals of the schools studied were asked to indicate the attitude of their teachers toward postgraduate students in their classes. Seventy-nine per cent of the principals replied that their teachers did not object to having these students in their classes, twelve per cent reported that the teachers preferred them, and only eight per cent reported that their teachers disliked this type of student. A few of the principals volunteered the information that caring for postgraduate students in large regular classes often requires a great amount of extra work on the part of the teachers, which causes a dislike for such students. If it were possible to provide better facilities, many of these teachers would probably change their attitude.

The principals were also asked to report the attitude of their undergraduate students toward the postgraduate students. Forty-three per cent of the principals reported that their undergraduate students were indifferent to the postgraduates, fifty-two per cent that postgraduates were readily accepted, and five per cent that their undergraduates did not want these students in the school.

On the whole, the attitude of the administration, teachers, and students, as reported by the high school principals, was favorable toward postgraduate students.

The school attitude and its relation to the postgraduate enrollment of the schools studied are shown in Table X. The mean

TABLE X

RELATIONSHIP BETWEEN SCHOOL ATTITUDE TOWARD POSTGRADUATES AND
NUMBER OF SCHOOLS REPORTING POSTGRADUATES IN THE SCHOOL

NUMBER OF POSTGRADUATES	NUMBER OF SCHOOLS THAT ENCOURAGE POST- GRADUATES	NUMBER OF SCHOOLS THAT HAVE NO POLICY	NUMBER OF SCHOOLS THAT DISCOURAGE POST- GRADUATES
65–above	4	4	0
60–64	0	1	0
55–59	0	1	0
50–54	0	3	0
45–49	0	1	0
40–44	1	6	0
35–39	1	6	1
30–34	2	2	2
25–29	2	6	0
20–24	6	11	1
15–19	6	10	2
10–14	12	26	3
5– 9	32	48	6
0– 4	61	104	13

number of postgraduates for the schools in which these students are encouraged is twelve, and the mean for the schools having no policy is sixteen. The schools discouraging postgraduates have a mean of four students.

The larger number of schools studied do not discourage postgraduates officially, but are these same schools consistent in their rules and regulations and in their provision for the educational opportunities for these students?

To get a complete picture of the attitude of public high schools toward postgraduate students, one must not only examine the officially expressed attitudes, but also the rules and regulations governing these students. It is quite possible for a school to encourage students of this class officially, yet to set up restrictions which would make attendance unpleasant or unprofitable because of the lack of educational opportunities.

One set of rules which affects postgraduates is that which determines the periods of daily attendance required. Of the five hundred twenty-five schools studied, fifty-nine per cent have such regulations. Nineteen per cent insist that the student must attend school full time regardless of the number of studies he takes. On the other hand, the larger number of schools, or sixty-one per cent, have ruled that the student need be in school only for the periods he is actually in class. Fourteen per cent reported that the postgraduate must attend school half a day, while a small proportion, or five per cent, set other minimum numbers of periods of attendance. The number of schools for each type of attendance restriction is compared with the postgraduate enrollment in Table XI. The mean postgraduate enrollment for full-day attendance is twelve; for the actual number of periods of class work, eleven; for half-day attendance, eight; and for other minimum periods of attendance, twenty-three. The attendance requirements cannot be said to affect materially the number of postgraduate students in a school. The difference in the mean number of postgraduates under a full-time requirement and the periods in class requirement is only one. When the reasons why high school graduates return for study are examined, in the next chapter, it is noted that about eighty per cent return either to make up credit for college entrance, to secure specific vocational training, or to be occupied until employment is found. Students coming back for these purposes can usually attend full time and consequently would not be affected by the attendance restrictions mentioned. Two schools volunteered the information that inasmuch as all their postgraduates came back for only a period or

TABLE XI

RELATIONSHIP OF THE NUMBER OF SCHOOLS HAVING ATTENDANCE REQUIRE-
MENTS FOR POSTGRADUATES AND THE POSTGRADUATE ENROLLMENT

NUMBER OF POSTGRADUATES	SCHOOL ATTENDANCE REQUIREMENTS			
	Full Day	Periods in Class	Half Day	Other Minimum Periods
65–above	3	2	0	2
60–64	0	2	0	0
55–59	0	2	0	0
50–54	0	1	0	1
45–49	0	0	0	0
40–44	1	4	1	0
35–39	2	4	1	1
30–34	2	1	0	1
25–29	0	3	3	1
20–24	2	15	1	1
15–19	6	11	1	0
10–14	9	22	10	1
5– 9	17	57	9	4
0– 4	19	67	20	3
Total	61	191	46	15

two of work, they encouraged these students to seek outside employment in addition to their school work.

There is one other administrative regulation which is more strict for postgraduate students than for regular students; that is, the one which requires the former class of students to maintain a certain standard of scholarship to remain in school. Two hundred twenty-one schools out of five hundred twenty-five, or forty-two per cent, have such a rule. This standard is reported by these schools to be "a passing grade," or "seventy per cent," or "C." This passing grade is not different from that set for the undergraduate student. The difference is that failure on the part of the postgraduate will result in his being dropped from school, whereas the undergraduate is not dropped but carried on or changed to another subject. The principal of one school made the statement which summarizes the policy behind this regulation, and that is, "The postgraduate student comes back to get definite work. Unless he can make good in that he had better drop out."

These attendance restrictions are closely related to the number of subjects which postgraduates take and which will be discussed in greater detail in the following chapter. In the larger number of cases, this type of student takes only one or two subjects. The purpose of the restrictions has been to permit him to get what he wants, and yet not loaf in school when he is finished with his work. The sixty-one schools requiring full-day attendance insist that the postgraduate shall take a full program of subjects.

There is no relationship between the size of the schools studied or the size of the postgraduate enrollment and these particular regulations.

CURRICULAR OPPORTUNITIES AVAILABLE FOR POSTGRADUATE STUDENTS

The curricular opportunities available for postgraduates are ordinarily determined by the needs of the undergraduate and usually limited to the curriculum of the undergraduate. In the previous section the statement was made that the principals reported that eighty per cent of their postgraduates returned to make up college entrance credits, to receive specific vocational training, or to keep occupied until employment is available. Into what courses do these students go to satisfy their needs?

These students either desire college preparatory subjects or specialized vocational subjects, such as are found in commercial or trade curricula. The principals of the schools studied were asked to report the curricula in their schools in which the dominant number of postgraduates enrolled. It will be seen from Table XII, which shows the relationship between the size of the postgraduate enrollment and the curricula in which the dominant postgraduate enrollment exists, that two hundred seven schools reported the larger number of their postgraduates in the college preparatory curriculum, whereas two hundred sixteen schools reported that their dominant enrollment is in the commercial curriculum. The mean postgraduate enrollment for the college preparatory curriculum is thirteen, while the mean enrollment in the commercial curriculum is twelve.

Another aspect of this situation is brought out in Table XII, which shows the relationship between sizes of the schools studied and the number of schools having dominant postgraduate enroll-

TABLE XII

RELATIONSHIP OF SIZE OF THE POSTGRADUATE ENROLLMENT WITH NUMBER OF
SCHOOL CURRICULA IN WHICH DOMINANT POSTGRADUATE
ENROLLMENT EXISTS

NUMBER OF POSTGRADUATES	DOMINANT COURSES					
	College Preparatory	Commercial	General	Art	Trade	Total
65–above	6	5	2	0	1	14
60–64	1	2	0	0	0	3
55–59	2	1	0	0	0	3
50–54	1	0	0	0	0	1
45–49	1	1	0	0	0	2
40–44	5	5	0	2	0	12
35–39	4	3	0	0	1	8
30–34	6	4	1	1	0	12
25–29	5	6	1	1	1	14
20–24	12	14	3	1	1	31
15–19	14	12	2	0	2	30
10–14	33	31	6	0	2	72
5– 9	62	56	16	4	2	140
0– 4	55	76	16	0	5	152
Total	207	216	47	9	15	494

TABLE XIII

RELATIONSHIP BETWEEN SIZES OF SCHOOLS STUDIED AND NUMBER OF SCHOOLS
HAVING DOMINANT ENROLLMENTS IN CERTAIN CURRICULA

SIZE OF SCHOOL	DOMINANT COURSES						
	College Preparatory	Commercial	General	Art	Trade	Other	Total
4,000–above	7	4	1	2	0	0	14
3,500–3,999	5	4	1	1	0	0	11
3,000–3,499	5	5	5	0	0	0	15
2,500–2,999	8	4	0	1	1	0	14
2,000–2,499	22	16	3	1	1	0	43
1,500–1,999	20	20	2	2	0	0	44
1,000–1,499	36	35	12	0	3	0	86
500– 999	69	68	15	2	8	0	162
0– 499	63	93	18	3	5	2	184
Total	235	249	57	12	18	2	573

ments in certain curricula. The significant feature brought out in this table is that for practically every size level there are schools which have dominant postgraduate enrollments in the college preparatory and commercial curricula. The curricula, then, into which most postgraduates go, and which are offered more generally, are the college preparatory and the commercial. These two curricula are extensive and include many subjects. However, all the subjects in the college preparatory and commercial curricula are not open to the postgraduates; some schools close certain classes to students returning for extra work.

What subjects are closed to the postgraduate? Eighty-one, or fifteen per cent, of the schools studied have definitely closed certain classes to the student who comes back. Seventy of these schools have excluded postgraduates from their freshmen and sophomore classes, with a few exceptions. Some of these exceptions are advanced algebra, bookkeeping, language, geometry, or other subjects which may be essential for college entrance. Then, again, commercial subjects may be excepted. Some high schools go further in their limitations, as, for example, the Senior High School at Artesia, New Mexico, which closes "all classes except those strictly commercial subjects and solid geometry for college entrance."[19] Other schools, instead of specifying subjects which are closed to the student who comes back, indicate subjects by grades, as is the case of the High School at Braintree, Massachusetts, which has ruled that first-year English and second-year English are limited to undergraduates. Five of the schools give the undergraduates first opportunity to enroll in classes.

The size of the school has no bearing on this regulation. Small schools as well as large are included in the group of schools which close classes to the postgraduate.

Although some schools close certain classes to postgraduates, others require that certain subjects be taken. Twelve schools reported such practices. Three of these schools require that English be taken; one requires health education; two require physical education; and two require postgraduates to take commercial work if they desire to return to high school. On the other hand, one school requires that academic work be taken if the student plans to come back. Greene High School of Greene, New

[19] Communicated to the writer, February 1931.

York, requires its postgraduates to take some English, and they must carry one more subject than the regular student; whereas one of the high schools of Yonkers, New York, requires that students who come back must take subjects not carried before.

These twelve schools vary in size. One has two hundred students; one has five hundred; two have twelve hundred; the next, fourteen hundred; then, one with seventeen hundred; and the remaining five have enrollments exceeding twenty-five hundred. The mean number of postgraduates for this group of schools is twelve. Thus, size of school and number of postgraduates do not relate to the rule that postgraduates take certain subjects.

It should be pointed out that, although the returning students are required to take these subjects, these particular schools do not adapt the work especially to them. However, a few schools, nine out of the five hundred twenty-five, or about one per cent, have made serious efforts to set up work intended for and adapted to postgraduate students. For instance, the Central High School of Manchester, New Hampshire, offers a typewriting course exclusively for postgraduates.

Large numbers of the postgraduates, as will be considered later, return and take up subjects different from their major interest. For example, college preparatory students take up a few commercial subjects, not because they plan to follow this as a vocation but because they feel it may be helpful in their later college or professional work. In this connection, Principal W. Y. Morrison, Headmaster of Central High School, writes:

> The typewriting which we offer exclusively to postgraduates is the same work we offer to undergraduate students. The postgraduates in this case, however, are pupils drawn from the Classical and General Courses in which typewriting is not offered. The reason we do not combine the postgraduates with the undergraduates is that we find the postgraduates can move at a faster pace and cover more ground, probably due to longer school experience and a deeper incentive for the work taken.

The John Marshall High School, Richmond, Virginia, has also set up work intended for and adapted to postgraduates. Commercial courses are planned especially for students going into the commercial field. The principal, James C. Harwood, writes:

> An intensive course in Shorthand, Typewriting, and Business Methods should be offered for graduates who did not take the Commercial Course

but must enter the business field. This course should be ungraded and should require no specified time to complete. It should be open only to graduates, who should be allowed to work at capacity till properly prepared. It would require the full time of one teacher, two additional rooms, and necessary equipment.

In the New Haven High School, New Haven, Connecticut, separate English courses are provided for postgraduates, with emphasis on the enrichment of the senior English course and also on the individual problems in composition. Principal C. L. Kirschner states:

For convenience and in order to separate the postgraduates from the regular seniors, we have established regular English courses for the postgraduates. This is possible as practically all carry English. Next year we expect to add other classes for postgraduates exclusively, if enough register to make up a division.

In general the English for the postgraduates follows the Senior course with some enrichment and with more intensive study on some authors or lines of work. In composition, attention is given to individual problems such as drill in fundamentals, development of imagination, and self-expression.

The High School at Concord, New Hampshire, is a typical example. The students who are planning to take College Board Examinations go into the regular classes, as do the commercial students. Of special interest is the English course which is offered to a group of these students. Headmaster C. F. Cook describes his postgraduate program as follows:

The work which we give our postgraduate students depends entirely upon what the student wishes to do. Those who come back for the purpose of completing college requirements must necessarily take the work which leads to that end and so are placed in our regular senior divisions. This is especially true of those who are preparing for the College Board Examinations.

The graduates of the commercial course usually return for the purpose of going into classes and keeping up speed in stenography. They remain usually until they find a good position.

This present semester we have had a larger number of postgraduates than we have ever had before—more than twice as many, in fact, due probably to unemployment conditions largely.

For one division of these postgraduates, we have arranged a different type of work. We were fortunate in having a teacher free who could do this. The following quotation from a statement by the teacher in charge gives the content and aim of the course:

"The course we are now offering the postgraduates is a survey of English literature from Beowulf to the present time.

"As many of the classics have already been studied intensively, our aim in this course is not only to furnish a further cultural background, but also to try to arouse such an interest in the student that he will do further reading by himself.

"However, if the request comes from a student, as it has quite often, that more time be allowed for critical study of some selection, we welcome it as a sign that we are accomplishing something we had hoped for.

"In our reading, the study of the literature itself with its social and political background is emphasized rather than a study of the author's life.

"The state and city libraries have generously coöperated with us, laying out reference books which the students are urged, though not required, to consult.

"From time to time a theme is required which compels considerable research.

"The selections which we use are found in *Twelve Centuries of English Poetry and Prose,* Newcomer, Andrews, Hall.

"A copy of *A History of English Literature,* Neilson and Thorndike, is in the hands of each pupil and he is urged to carry that along as hour reading.

"We are able to do this work in this manner this semester but whether the increasing number of undergraduates will allow us the opportunity next year, we cannot now tell. However, if the postgraduates return next year as they are doing now we shall plan some such work as we are doing now. It is something different from the undergraduate courses which they have had and we think will bring increased interest and better results."

English work is specially adapted to the students who return to the Glenville High School of Cleveland, Ohio. Here the work is largely individual. Miss Laura J. Edwards, Head of the English Department, describes the work as follows:

The work we offer our graduate pupils is largely individual, although a few units are done by the group as a whole. The work consists in part of readings selected from the chosen lists. The pupils have done some Bible reading following an outline of Old Testament History, including material on the books of the Bible of special literary interest. The rest of the course consists mainly of magazine reading. The magazines used are the *Reader's Digest, Harpers, The Forum, The Atlantic,* and *Scribner's.*

English V and French IV are offered especially in Columbia High School, South Orange, New Jersey. Morris High School in New York City and Lincoln High School in Los Angeles offer commercial subjects with emphasis on shorthand and typing for postgraduates. Greene High School, Greene, New York, offers work that is related to teacher training and is intended for students going into that phase of work.

These schools which are giving special attention to postgraduates can, with one exception, be called large schools with a large number of postgraduates, as is shown in Table XIV. The mean

TABLE XIV

HIGH SCHOOLS OFFERING SUBJECTS INTENDED EXCLUSIVELY FOR POSTGRADUATE
STUDENTS

SCHOOL	LOCATION	ENROLL-MENT	NUMBER OF POST-GRADUATES	SUBJECT OR CURRICULUM
Central	Manchester, N. H.	1,863	35	Typing
John Marshall	Richmond, Va.	3,783	0	Shorthand, typing
New Haven	New Haven, Conn.	4,100	50	English
Concord	Concord, N. H.	853	38	English
Glenville	Cleveland, Ohio	1,773	24	English
Columbia	S. Orange, N. J.	1,150	17	English V French IV
Morris	New York City	5,665	179	Commercial
Lincoln	Los Angeles, Calif.	2,500	90	Commercial
Greene	Greene, N. Y.	205	14	Pre-teacher-training

enrollment for this group of schools is two thousand thirty-two, while the mean postgraduate enrollment is fifty. The subjects are divided rather evenly between English and Commercial, with one French and one pre-teacher-training course. It must be remembered that providing special subjects for these students implies teacher time, rooms, and equipment. There must be a sufficient number enrolled to warrant this expense. In the schools mentioned this was the case.

In this section in which the educational opportunities available for postgraduates are considered, it will be noted that the college preparatory and commercial curricula absorb the larger number of these students. These curricula appear in practically all the schools studied regardless of size or number of postgraduates. It is found, further, that in about fifteen per cent of the schools studied certain subjects are closed to postgraduates, these being largely in grades nine and ten.   Two per cent of the schools require that certain subjects be taken, but only one per cent of the schools studied offer subjects set up exclusively for postgraduate students.   In this last group of schools, English and commercial subjects are offered most frequently.

EDUCATIONAL OPPORTUNITIES OFFERED IN EXTRACURRICULAR ACTIVITIES

In the previous section the educational opportunities offered postgraduates through the curricula of the high school were reviewed.   In addition to these, there is another important part of the school program, namely, the extracurricular activities.

The practices vary in different high schools as to whether or not postgraduates may participate in the various extracurricular activities.   The principals of the schools studied were asked to indicate whether the students who returned were admitted to all extracurricular activities, to none at all, or to a limited number.

Three hundred nine schools reported on this subject.   Twenty-six per cent of the schools open all their activities to postgraduates, forty-four per cent close all activities to these students, while the remaining twenty-nine per cent permit this group of students to participate in a limited number of activities.   The mean number of postgraduates in schools where all activities are open is twelve; the mean number of postgraduates in the schools which close their activities is thirteen; and the schools limiting the number of activities have a mean number of nine students.   An examination of Table XV shows that the prohibiting of extracurricular activities has not affected the postgraduate enrollment in the schools.   In fact, the schools in which the prohibition exists have a slightly higher mean postgraduate enrollment than the group of schools in which the activities are open.

In the group of schools which limits the activities in which postgraduates may participate, the activities for which they are eligible are mentioned.   These activities are listed in the order of their frequency as follows: band, orchestra, and music; intramural sports, with a definite provision that the student is not to represent the school on any varsity or interschool team; school clubs; dramatics; journalism (i.e., he may contribute to school papers and magazines) ; certain minor offices in minor activities;

TABLE XV

RELATIONSHIP BETWEEN POSTGRADUATE ENROLLMENT AND NUMBER OF HIGH
SCHOOLS EXPRESSING POLICIES IN EXTRACURRICULAR ACTIVITIES

NUMBER OF POSTGRADUATES	NUMBER OF SCHOOLS WITH E.C.A. OPEN TO P.G.	NUMBER OF SCHOOLS WITH E.C.A. CLOSED TO P.G.	NUMBER OF SCHOOLS WITH E.C.A. LIMITED TO P.G.	TOTAL
65–above	1	5	2	8
60–64	0	2	0	2
55–59	1	0	0	1
50–54	1	1	0	2
45–49	0	0	0	0
40–44	2	4	1	7
35–39	1	5	0	6
30–34	4	1	1	6
25–29	2	1	3	6
20–24	5	10	4	19
15–19	4	7	5	16
10–14	14	15	8	37
5– 9	20	39	30	89
0– 4	25	48	37	110
Total	80	138	91	309

NOTE.—In the above table the letters E. C. A. represent extracurricular activities, and P. G., postgraduates.

assemblies, with permission to participate occasionally; and debates. One school opens its general class social functions to the postgraduate. Small schools and large ones, as well as medium sized schools, are represented in all three groups.

The home-room or major-room programs are often considered part of the extracurricular plan of a high school. It is for that reason that the home-room opportunities of the postgraduate students are presented here.

The principals of three hundred twenty-one schools give information which shows that in fifty-nine per cent of these schools the postgraduates are assigned to home rooms with seniors; in twenty-one per cent of the schools they are assigned to rooms wherever there may be vacancies; and in nineteen per cent of the cases they are assigned to home rooms made up exclusively of postgraduate students. These figures are significant only to show that the assignment of these students to home rooms other than those for postgraduates practically prevents any special home-room programs from being carried on for these students.

Sixteen schools, or three per cent of those studied, indicate that special home-room programs are carried on. Four of the schools, the Garfield in Los Angeles, California, the Polytechnic in San Francisco, California, the high school at Santa Barbara, California, and the high school at Hartford, Connecticut, provide vocational and educational guidance. The other schools reported varying activities, such as the Lincoln High School, Detroit, Michigan, which organizes its postgraduate home room for social activities, and the Washington High School, Portland, Oregon, which reports that its postgraduates are planning to publish an annual at the end of this present term, which is the first attempt at any special venture. The high school at Hartford, Connecticut, reported that its postgraduates are organized as a postgraduate club and carry on a program of general interest to this club, such as conducting sales of Christmas cards for the benefit of the school scholarship fund. The Arsenal Technical High School, Indianapolis, Indiana, reported that its postgraduates "conduct distinctive service activities for the school."

Is it the large school or the small school which is giving special home-room programs for postgraduates? The sixteen schools represent all sizes of schools. These schools range in size from one hundred to four thousand.

In examining the program of extracurricular activities, it is noted in seventy per cent of the schools that there is either no participation or participation in a limited number of activities. Several principals volunteered the reason for this policy. These students come back for a specific purpose. They want one or two subjects and the schools are concerned with meeting their expressed needs. In the matter of home-room programs adapted to students of this group, there are only three per cent of the schools making any attempt to enlarge the educational opportunities of the postgraduate students by this instrument. Most postgraduate students are deprived of the educational opportunities provided undergraduates through the extracurricular activities.

SPECIAL LIBRARY AND STUDY-HALL PRIVILEGES

A phase of the educational opportunities offered postgraduate students is the special library and study-hall privileges extended to these students.

Five per cent of the schools give the postgraduates library privileges which are not extended to the undergraduate students. These privileges are of three types: one, they may go to the library without restriction; two, they may use the library unsupervised; and three, they may keep books for a longer period of time. This is evidence that the postgraduate student is being given more freedom. This is better brought out in some of the schools which follow this practice. The High School of Amherst, Massachusetts, permits the postgraduates to use the library without the usual pass required of other students; in the High School at Clarksburg, West Virginia, they use the library unsupervised; postgraduates are only required to attend classes for which they are enrolled, in the High School at Franklin, New Hampshire, and so may use the library at will; and in the High School at Menasha, Wisconsin, they are permitted to keep books a longer time. The Oliver High School of Pittsburgh, Pennsylvania, gives its postgraduates the same privileges as the other students with the exception that these special students may have more time in the library. This last privilege is the one most commonly practiced. The postgraduate, in the larger number of cases, takes but one or two classes. He is, therefore, permitted to use the library as much as he desires.

Closely associated with the extension of library privileges is the granting of study-hall privileges. These study-hall privileges are of two types: one, the student may go to the library or some other place to work instead of to the study hall; and two, after finishing classes he may leave the building or otherwise do as he wishes.

Thirty schools extend study-hall privileges to the postgraduate. There is a tendency to make the postgraduate a free agent in these schools. For instance, the High School at Cloquet, Minnesota, allows postgraduates "to come and go at pleasure"; at Lawrence High School, Falmouth, Massachusetts, they have "more freedom to come and go"; Franklin High School, Franklin, Massachusetts, requires the student "to attend classes only; may use study hall at will"; at Las Vegas, Nevada, "they are allowed to come and go as they choose"; and at the High School at Willcox, Arizona, they are "at liberty to study at school or at home. No study-hall checks are kept on them." At White Plains

High School, White Plains, New York, requirements are a little more rigid. Here, "there is a room definitely set aside as a place for the postgraduate to study. They do not go to regular study halls." However, only five per cent of the schools studied extend special library and study-hall privileges to the postgraduates.

THE POSTGRADUATE AND HIGHER INSTITUTIONS

In the next chapter it will be shown that over fifty per cent of the postgraduates plan to go on to colleges and universities after they have completed their work in the high school. It is evident, therefore, that in a study of postgraduates this aspect of the problem must be considered. In Table XVI figures indicating the number of postgraduates who could have, and who could not have, lived at home while attending institutions of higher learning are presented.

TABLE XVI

RELATIONSHIP BETWEEN NUMBER OF POSTGRADUATES AND NUMBER OF SCHOOLS WITH POSTGRADUATE STUDENTS WHO WOULD HAVE TO LEAVE HOME TO ATTEND INSTITUTIONS OF HIGHER LEARNING

POSTGRADUATES	COULD LIVE AT HOME	COULD NOT LIVE AT HOME
65–above	6	1
60–64	1	1
55–59	1	1
50–54	2	0
45–49	1	0
40–44	5	2
35–39	8	1
30–34	5	1
25–29	7	1
20–24	13	3
15–19	16	1
10–14	26	13
5– 9	60	28
0– 4	75	30
Total	226	83

It is said that many parents prefer to keep their children under the influence of the home for a period longer than high school graduation requires, rather than send them away to a college. How many of the postgraduates studied could have attended college and lived at home? The principals of the schools studied were asked this question. Eighty-three, or twenty-seven per cent, of the schools giving information on this question, are so located that their postgraduate students would have to leave home if they were to attend an institution of higher learning. In seventy-three per cent of the schools it would be quite possible for these students to live at home and still attend college or some other institution of higher learning. The fact that these students did not attend some institution of higher learning was due to (a) not being eligible to attend; (b) inability to get the work desired; (c) was not old enough to be away from home. For the purposes of this study, an "institution of higher learning" is interpreted as an institution offering work beyond the twelfth grade.

The schools studied reported whether or not their graduates could enter the outstanding colleges and universities in their states upon certification of graduation. Thirty-five per cent reported that their students could not, but sixty-five per cent answered that their students could enter upon presenting a certificate of graduation. The fact that the graduates of a high school were not accepted in colleges of the state upon certificates of graduation did not affect the postgraduate enrollment in the schools studied.

Twenty-six per cent of the schools reported that postgraduate work is not accepted for entrance credit by some of the colleges and universities in their states. This did not reduce the number of postgraduates who planned to attend college when their work was completed. It was explained by two principals that the students who take postgraduate studies and wish to have them accepted for entrance credit apply for admission to colleges which will recognize this work. Again, there are many postgraduates who have sufficient credit so that it is not necessary for them to ask for entrance credit on their postgraduate work.

Closely associated with the problem of college-entrance credit is the problem of granting advanced credit by colleges and universities. Eighty-one per cent of the schools reported that colleges have given advanced credit to a few of their students in the past.

Letters were sent to all the state universities and to twenty additional leading colleges and universities, a total of sixty-five institutions, to get their points of view. Sixty-two universities and colleges answered. They are very definite and positive in their policy of granting advanced credit for work taken in high school as a postgraduate student. Fifty-four per cent stated that under no circumstances is advanced credit given. Thirty-four per cent reported that advanced credit may be given in unusual circumstances after an examination set up by the departments concerned has been passed, but this is not to be interpreted as being the regular practice of those institutions. Eleven per cent may, under special conditions, give credit without examinations. These seven institutions are the University of Illinois, which may give advanced credit in algebra and trigonometry where the mathematics departments have been particularly strong in the high school; Rhode Island State College; University of Mississippi; University of California; Marquette University, which gives advanced credit only for English students who have had trigonometry; University of Nevada; and Oberlin College, which gives advanced credit in English, French, Spanish, Latin, Greek, history, social sciences, mathematics, and physical sciences.

The institutions of higher learning may be said to stimulate postgraduate enrollment by either discouraging or not providing for matriculation in the spring semester. The one hundred four schools considered in the first chapter that had an increased spring postgraduate enrollment owing to students who either could not or felt that it was not wise to enter college at the close of the fall semester, is a fact in point. This type of student has three possible choices: first, to stay at home; second, to seek employment; and third, to take postgraduate work at the high school. In the present economic situation, the opportunities for employment are not numerous and so the student who cannot secure a position comes back to school. Many of the spring postgraduates have gained a semester due to superior ability, or have lost a semester through slowness, sickness or some other cause which kept them out of school. In this group, also, are those who entered the high school in the second semester. It should be possible for these students to carry work which will be recognized and will aid their progress toward their vocational objective. There are two solutions: one, to have the colleges and universities give advanced credit after proper verification of postgraduate work; or second, to eliminate semiannual promotions in the high school and enrich the program of the superior pupil. Two principals stated that they were seriously considering following this second plan.

PLACEMENT OPPORTUNITIES FOR POSTGRADUATES

A supplementary part of the educational program for the postgraduate student is the opportunity for placement. Forty-eight per cent of the schools studied indicated that the larger number of their postgraduates go directly into employment.

One hundred thirty-nine of the schools, or twenty-six per cent, reported that they have placement services which help the postgraduate student to secure employment. These services, set up for all the students in the school, are managed by various members of the staff such as the principal, the vice-principal, the counselor, or in some cases, the home-room teacher. Students going into the same fields of work as their fathers often receive placement help in these fields.

Twenty-seven per cent of the schools studied reported that it is easier to place postgraduate students than regular high school graduates, owing to the further intensive work they receive. If commercial work on the postgraduate level makes it easier for these students to receive positions, it would appear to argue for more commercial work above the twelfth-grade level. On the other hand, two per cent of the schools indicated that it is more difficult to secure positions for postgraduates.

It is particularly significant that as many as one hundred thirty-nine schools have made arrangements to aid their postgraduate students in placements. This placement service has developed as the vocational subjects have been brought into the school. However, in seventy-one per cent of the schools there is no organized placement service available to the postgraduate student.

SUMMARY

Although the majority of state superintendents are not hostile to the provision of educational opportunities for the postgraduate student, no state makes any direct legal provision for such privileges. The matter is left entirely in the hands of the local boards of education, with a few states setting up minor regulations. In the five hundred twenty-five schools studied, it was found that only eight per cent definitely discourage their high school graduates from returning for additional work. It happens that the schools without an expressed policy have the largest number of postgraduate students of this class. Fifty-nine per cent of the schools studied limit the attendance of the postgraduate to the number of periods of actual classroom instruction. Certain subjects and classes, chiefly those in grades nine and ten, are closed to students of this type in fifteen per cent of the schools, whereas twelve per cent of the schools require that certain subjects be taken, such as English and physical education. Practically all schools indicated that their dominant enrollments were in the college preparatory and commercial curricula. One per cent of the schools have set up subjects adapted to and exclusively for postgraduates. These subjects are English, typing, and shorthand. The mean postgraduate enrollment for this group of schools (i.e., schools with large enrollments) is fifty. The extracurricular activities which are open to all undergraduate students are either closed or limited in the case of postgraduates in seventy-three per cent of the schools. A very small number of schools, only five per cent, extend library or study-hall privileges to students of this type. Although seventy-four per cent of the schools report that institutions of higher learning will accept postgraduate work for entrance, only eleven per cent of the colleges and universities indicate that they will give advanced credit for this type of work without examinations, and even in these cases the regulations are restrictive. The postgraduate enrollment increases in the spring each year because the high school graduate feels that his college opportunities are limited by spring matriculation.

In twenty-seven per cent of the schools it was found easier to place students who had had postgraduate work than regular high school graduates. In other schools it was felt that coming back for postgraduate work did not make it any easier for the schools to secure employment for these students.

Although direct evidence does not show it, one examining the check lists from the schools studied realizes the fact that postgraduates are not welcomed in most of the schools studied. The regulation of attendance, closed classes, required classes, and the extracurricular limitations, as well as the attitude of higher institutions toward giving advanced credit for this type of work, all tend to discourage postgraduate students. The fact that the postgraduate enrollment is increasing in spite of lack of encouragement and educational provisions in the public high schools is significant. There is a growing demand for educational opportunities beyond the twelfth grade by an increasing number of high school graduates, those who are delaying college entrance for one reason or another, as well as those who need specific vocational training. In this connection it may be pointed out again that there is a marked tendency for postgraduate enrollments to be low in high schools in communities where there are satisfactory junior college opportunities.

CHAPTER III

THE POSTGRADUATE STUDENT

NATURE OF THE INVESTIGATION OF THE POSTGRADUATE
STUDENT

Turning from a consideration of the educational opportunities available for postgraduate students one should study the traits and characteristics of these students themselves. This is necessary to determine whether or not these educational opportunities really meet the needs of the postgraduate student. The facts used in the previous chapter were obtained from the principals of five hundred twenty-five representative schools. The information used as a basis for this chapter was secured by studying the postgraduates in a selected number of these schools.

In the previous chapter it was brought out that of the total number replying, three hundred thirty-four of the schools reported postgraduate students enrolled. A check list to be filled out by postgraduate students was sent to high schools in fifty-five different communities.

This check list requested facts from the postgraduate dealing with his background, his high school educational history, his plans for the future, and the subjects and school activities in which he was then participating. In addition to this, the principal of the school was asked to give information concerning each student in the senior class; namely, his scholastic rank and his intelligence score or quotient on any one of the standardized intelligence tests he may have taken.

Schools in fifty-two communities in twenty-three different states sent in check lists on eleven hundred sixty-nine postgraduates. Each of these communities reported one high school, with the exception of Springfield, Massachusetts, which reported three, and Detroit, Michigan, which reported two. The fact that about one-third of the postgraduates in this study come from Springfield and Detroit does not give undue weight to any of the characteristics of this group of students. The postgraduate students in these two cities were similar in their chief characteristics to the postgraduate students from the schools in the other cities studied. This applies to the intelligence quotients, the plans for the future, and the subjects in which the students were enrolled.

To bring out any traits or characteristics which might be peculiar to postgraduate students, a comparison was made between the postgraduates in eight high schools and a random selection of seniors in these schools. In every case at least fifty seniors were selected. The facts which formed the basis for the comparison were secured by means of a check list filled out by the senior students. This check list for the seniors requested facts concerning the student's background, the type of school work he was then taking, and his plans after graduation from high school. The principal was asked to furnish for each one of these students his scholastic rank in his class and the scores or quotients obtained on standardized intelligence tests.

Facts on nine hundred fifteen seniors were reported by eight schools located in the following communities: Springfield, Massachusetts; Syracuse, New York; Detroit, Michigan; New Haven, Connecticut; Tulsa, Oklahoma; and Hartford, Connecticut.

To make the intelligence test quotients obtained from different tests comparable, they were equated in terms of Terman Group Test of Mental Ability, Form A, by the method described and applied by Dr. Grayson N. Kefauver.[1] The equation was made in terms of the Terman quotient because seventy per cent of the six hundred eleven postgraduates for whom intelligence test scores were received had been given this particular test. The other tests represented were the Dearborn Group Intelligence Test, Series II C, Illinois General Intelligence Scale, Form I, Otis Self-Administering Test of Mental Ability, Higher and Intermediate, and the Haggerty, Delta 2.

The Kefauver tables which were used in making these scores equivalent to the Terman Group Test of Mental Ability were derived by what is known as the standard deviation procedure. These were worked out by determining the intelligence quotients obtained from different tests given to the same group of pupils which have similar standard-deviation positions.

[1] Kefauver, Grayson N. "Need of Equating Intelligence Quotients Obtained from Group Tests." *Journal of Educational Research*, Vol. III, pp. 92-101, February 1929.

THE PERSONAL CHARACTERISTICS OF THE POSTGRADUATE STUDENTS

The program for the postgraduate students should be developed in terms of the needs of the students served. The student's capacity for academic work must be considered, his age, whether he is employed while attending school, and his father's occupation. These are all factors which may or may not determine whether the student should come back for additional work.

Language difficulty may possibly present itself in connection with a student's capacity for academic work. Such difficulty may arise from the foreign birth of the student or of the father. However, the foreign birth of the postgraduate cannot be said to provide language difficulties for a majority of these students. Ninety-five per cent of the nine hundred eighty-five postgraduates studied were born in the United States, and two per cent of the remaining five claimed Canada as the country of birth. In examining the postgraduates and the seniors from the same schools, it is noted that the situation is practically the same except that one per cent more students are born abroad in the senior group.

The fact that the father is born outside the United States may appear significant in that it may indicate that a foreign language is used in the home, thus making it difficult for the child of the family to acquire sufficient mastery of English to do satisfactory work in high school. This, however, cannot be said to be a factor in the postgraduate problem. The fathers of seventy per cent of the postgraduates studied were born in the United States. The remaining thirty per cent of the postgraduates had fathers born in all countries of Europe and America, the larger number coming from Russia, Canada, England, Sweden, Germany, and Italy.

Many students find it necessary to work while they are attending high school. Twenty-seven per cent of the postgraduate students considered were working, the larger number being boys. The mean number of hours that the boys were employed was twenty-three, whereas that for the girls was twenty. Of the special group of postgraduates and seniors, the postgraduates worked an average of twenty-three hours a week and the seniors seventeen. The difference is very small. The postgraduate student, as will be shown later, carries but one of two subjects, whereas the seniors average four and in some cases, five. Although the postgraduate has more time to work, there is no evidence to show that postgraduates as a group carry a heavier load in outside employment than the senior students. The mean intelligence quotient, as measured or stated in terms of Terman's Intelligence Test, of six hundred eleven postgraduates is one hundred eight (see Table XVII), with a range

TABLE XVII

DISTRIBUTION OF 611 POSTGRADUATES AND 915 SENIORS ACCORDING TO SEX AND INTELLIGENCE QUOTIENT

INTELLIGENCE QUOTIENT	POSTGRADUATES			SENIORS		
	Boys	Girls	Total Number	Boys	Girls	Total Number
145–above	3	1	4	3	2	5
140–144	1	3	4	4	2	6
135–139	4	1	5	11	6	17
130–134	8	7	15	13	14	27
125–129	13	14	27	27	17	44
120–124	24	10	34	29	27	56
115–119	71	48	119	60	82	142
110–114	53	38	91	58	77	135
105–109	45	43	88	59	82	141
100–104	31	36	67	53	62	115
95– 99	34	35	69	50	53	103
90– 94	13	17	30	25	42	67
85– 89	15	7	22	8	21	29
80– 84	8	6	14	7	12	19
75– below	17	5	22	3	6	9
Total	340	271	611	410	505	915

Mean Intelligence Quotient for Total Postgraduates	108.39
Mean Intelligence Quotient for Total Seniors	109.10
The Standard Error of Mean of Postgraduate Students	.540
The Standard Error of Mean of Senior Students	.425
The Standard Error of Difference Between the Two Means	.687

from one hundred sixty to forty-five. The mean intelligence quotient of the senior group is one hundred nine. The difference between the means for the senior and postgraduate groups is .71 with a standard error of .687. Since the standard error of the difference is practically as large as the difference, the intelligence of the two groups of students may be considered to be equivalent.

Practically all the schools studied measured the academic achievement of their students by ranking them in senior classes. When the rankings which the postgraduates had as seniors are considered (Table XVIII), it will be seen that the postgraduate group is practically representative of the total senior group. Fifty-three per cent of the postgraduates were in the upper half in intelligence, while half of the seniors were on this level. The largest variation is represented in the first quarter where thirty per cent of the postgraduates are located in comparison with the twenty-five per cent for the total senior class. The ranking of the seniors naturally places twenty-five per cent in each of the quarter groups.

TABLE XVIII

Class Rankings of 378 Postgraduate Students Compared with 330 Senior Students

Class Rank	Per Cent of Total Number of Postgraduates in Each Rank (330 Cases)
First Quarter	30
Second Quarter	23
Third Quarter	23
Fourth Quarter	22

In considering the per cent of boys in the fourth quarter for both postgraduates and seniors (data not reported) the per cent is largest for the seniors. It is apparent that some selection does take place as the group moves from the senior to the postgraduate level. As will be shown later in this chapter, the larger number of postgraduate boys take college preparatory subjects and are planning to go to college. However, the greater number of girls who come back for additional work go into the commercial curriculum. In this last group there are more students who rank low in academic achievement.

Since these students are advanced one year above seniors, one can expect them as a group to be older than the seniors. The mean age for the postgraduates is eighteen but the mean age for the seniors is seventeen. The range in the ages of the postgraduates is much greater than that for the members of the lower class. This range extends from fifteen years to thirty-six years, whereas the senior range extends from fourteen to twenty-three years. This shows that postgraduates are a more mature group than seniors. Seventy-one per cent of the postgraduates take up their work immediately after high school graduation. The mean age for this group is seventeen and one-half years, but the mean age for the thirteen per cent who return after one semester has elapsed is slightly over eighteen. For a four-semester interval, the mean age is nineteen and one-half years. The mean age for the group increases as the interval increases.

Professor George S. Counts in his study, *The Selective Character of American Secondary Education,* says, "Occupation is the central fact in the lives of the great masses of people." [2] The occupations of the fathers of the postgraduates, as well as the seniors, is considered in this study because it is another measure of selection. It may be said to determine the economic status of the family. The classification of the fathers is the same as that used by Counts in the study just mentioned. "This classification which takes the census classification as a basis goes further by breaking up the more complex groups and recognizing certain other groups. . . . The aim is to get classes of reasonable homogeneity from the standpoint of the social status, position in the economic order, and intellectual outlook." [3]

In the classification of proprietors are included bankers, landlords, merchants, shopkeepers, and the like, while in the group of professional service are included architects, lawyers, journalists, surgeons, teachers, and people in similar activities. Those included in managerial service are agents, foremen, officials, contractors, etc., while in the group included in commercial service, there are buyers, clerks in stores, salesmen, commercial travelers, and those engaged in like activities. Accountants, canvassers, clerks, collectors, etc., are classified under clerical service; and dairymen, fruit-growers, gardeners, ranchmen, etc., are classified under the heading of agricultural service. All artisans who own the shops in which they work are called artisan-proprietors, such as plumbers, printers, and tailors. The trade group needs no

[2] Counts, George S. *The Selective Character of American Secondary Education,* p. 21. University of Chicago Press, 1922.
[3] *Ibid.,* p. 22.

elaboration.   Neither does the transportation service nor the other classifications.

The classifications in Table XIX have been divided roughly for purposes of comparison into four groups.   This table shows that there is some difference in the occupational classifications of the fathers of seniors and postgraduates.   In classification A, there are thirteen per cent more fathers of postgraduates than of sen-

TABLE XIX

DISTRIBUTION OF 566 POSTGRADUATES AND 399 SENIORS IN THE SAME HIGH SCHOOLS, ACCORDING TO OCCUPATIONAL CLASSIFICATIONS OF FATHERS

OCCUPATIONAL CLASSIFICATIONS	PER CENT OF FATHERS OF POSTGRADUATES	PER CENT OF FATHERS OF SENIORS
A		
Proprietors	9	7
Professional service	13	8
Managerial service	13	10
Commercial service	11	8
Total	46	33
B		
Clerical service	6	7
Agricultural service	3	3
Artisan-proprietor	13	13
Total	22	23
C		
Building and related trades	5	9
Machine and related trades	6	8
Printing trade	1	2
Miscellaneous trades	4	7
Total	16	26
D		
Transportation service	5	6
Public service	4	5
Personal service	2	2
Mining, fishing, etc.	1	0
Common labor	4	3
Total	16	16

iors, or a difference of seventy-one per cent. The occupations in this group may be said to be those on a higher economic and social level than the others. In classification B there is little difference between the two groups, whereas in classification C there are ten per cent fewer fathers of postgraduates than fathers of seniors, or a difference of sixty-two per cent. The children of the skilled artisans are not as well represented in the postgraduate group. In the occupations under classification D there is little difference in the percentage of occupations.

In summarizing the characteristics of the background of the postgraduate students, it may be said that these students as a group come from American stock, that their fathers are alive, that it does not seem necessary for a large number of them to have outside paid employment, that they are chronologically older by a year than senior students, that they are equal to the seniors, as a group, in intelligence as measured by standardized intelligence tests and achievement rankings, and finally, that the majority come from homes where the father is in an occupational group which may be said to represent the higher economic and social level.

THE UNDERGRADUATE EDUCATIONAL HISTORY OF THE POSTGRADUATES

Turning from the factors which constitute a part of the personal characteristics of the postgraduates, the writer next examined the undergraduate educational history of these students. What subjects did they take as undergraduates? The subjects in the larger number of high schools are grouped into courses or curricula.

Table XX brings out the fact that there is little difference in the distribution of the postgraduates in the curricula in which they enrolled in the twelfth grade and in the lower grades. This table does not show the amount of individual change made by postgraduate students from curriculum to curriculum. An analysis of the data upon which this table is based reveals the fact that twenty-six per cent of these students were enrolled in one or more curricula different from those in which they were enrolled in their senior year. Eight per cent of the postgraduates changed curricula only once and this was when the senior year was reached. The change most common was from the general

TABLE XX

DISTRIBUTION OF 975 POSTGRADUATES ACCORDING TO CURRICULA FOLLOWED IN
GRADES NINE, TEN, AND ELEVEN, AND DURING THE TWELFTH GRADE

TYPE OF CURRICULUM	PER CENT OF POST-GRADUATES ENROLLED IN CURRICULA WHEN IN GRADES 9–11	PER CENT OF POST-GRADUATES ENROLLED IN CURRICULA WHEN IN GRADE 12
General	19	22
Academic	41	45
Scientific	11	9
Normal	1	1
Commercial	14	14
Fine arts	3	1
Industrial arts	3	3
Household arts	1	0
Agricultural	0	0
Others	2	2

to the commercial curricula and from the academic to the general. A total of one hundred eighty-five students had been enrolled in two or more curricula before the senior year was reached. This constituted eighteen per cent of the total number of postgraduates. The larger number of the postgraduates, seventy-four per cent of the total, kept the same curriculum through high school.

Closely associated is the question of the grade the students were in when they decided on the type of course or curriculum in which they were enrolled later as postgraduates. Twenty per cent of the postgraduates studied were enrolled in curricula which they had started in the ninth grade, while fifteen per cent were enrolled in curricula started in the senior year. Forty-nine per cent of these students were in curricula which had been started when they returned for postgraduate work. These facts will be considered again when a comparison is made between the subjects in which the postgraduate was enrolled as an undergraduate and the curricula enrolled in as a postgraduate.

In comparing the courses the postgraduates enrolled in as seniors and the courses the seniors were taking, Table XXI shows some differences. The significant differences are that twenty-nine per cent fewer senior students were enrolled in the general and

TABLE XXI

DISTRIBUTION OF 495 POSTGRADUATES AND 928 SENIORS IN THE SAME SCHOOLS
ACCORDING TO TYPE OF CURRICULA FOLLOWED DURING THE SENIOR
YEAR

TYPE OF CURRICULUM	PER CENT OF TOTAL OF POSTGRADUATE STUDENTS ENROLLED AS SENIORS (495 Cases)	PER CENT OF TOTAL OF SENIORS ENROLLED (928 Cases)
General	25	19
Academic	40	27
Scientific	7	17
Normal	0	1
Commercial	12	30
Fine arts	2	0
Industrial arts	4	0
Household arts	0	0
Agricultural	0	0
Others	4	1

academic courses, and more than twice as many of the seniors are in commercial courses.

THE VOCATIONAL AND EDUCATIONAL PLANS OF THE POSTGRADUATES

The vocational and educational plans of the postgraduates are closely associated with the reasons given for returning for postgraduate work. The fact is brought out in Table XXII that forty-eight per cent of the postgraduates return for additional work for reasons associated with institutions of higher learning. There are the winter class graduates who prefer to enter college in the fall. There is the twenty-five per cent who return to make up college entrance requirements. This group consists of not only those students who find it necessary to repeat the subject to raise their marks, but also that group of students who had not definitely decided upon their future until quite late in their high school careers, and thus did not have all the subjects necessary for college entrance.

In the previous section of this chapter, it was pointed out that sixty per cent of the postgraduates studied did not decide upon their postgraduate course or curriculum until their senior year or until after graduation. Then, there is that small group, or

TABLE XXII

DISTRIBUTION OF POSTGRADUATES ACCORDING TO REASONS FOR UNDERTAKING
POSTGRADUATE WORK

REASONS	BOYS	GIRLS	TOTAL	PER CENT OF TOTAL
Wait until September to enter college	108	84	192	16
Make up college entrance requirements	217	70	287	25
Get specific vocational training	49	110	159	13
Occupied until position opens	101	89	190	16
Not old enough to go to college	30	12	42	3
Attend school longer	19	10	29	2
Take up special work	32	53	85	7
Earn advanced college credit	57	16	73	6
Other reasons	34	50	84	7
Total	647	494	1,141	95

three per cent, who reported that they were not old enough to
attend college. Whether or not the student is old enough may be
the parents' decision or may be the regulation of the college or
university which the student plans to attend. Many colleges will
not accept students under sixteen years of age. However, parents
of students over this age may feel that their children should be
under the influence of the home longer.

Then there is the group which returns for specific vocational
training or to take up some special work. This group constitutes
twenty per cent of the entire group. It is significant that there
are about twice as many girls in this group as there are boys,
just the reverse of the college preparatory group. More boys
than girls decide to go to college as they approach the time of
high school graduation.

Six or seven high school principals, reporting on this phase of
the study, volunteered the information that this group of postgraduates was larger than it had ever been in the past, whereas
two principals indicated that although they have not had postgraduates in the past, the present economic situation was going
to force them to make provision for this group of students in
the future.

Students returning for postgraduate work for different purposes
have about the same intelligence quotient. Those waiting until

the fall to enter college have a mean intelligence quotient of one hundred eight; those not old enough to enter college, one hundred fifteen; and those making up college entrance requirements, one hundred six. The group returning for specific vocational training have a mean intelligence quotient of one hundred two; and those wishing to take up special work, one hundred four. The group waiting for employment to open up have a mean intelligence quotient of one hundred one. The groups with the highest intelligence quotients, then, were the young students who were not old enough to enter college and those who wished to enter college in the fall.

There is a relationship between the age of the postgraduates and the reason they returned for postgraduate work. This is especially noticeable in those reporting that they were not old enough to go to college. This group has a mean age of sixteen, with only two cases below sixteen. Next, in ascending order, are those who were waiting until fall to enter college and those who were earning advanced college credit. These two groups have a mean age of seventeen and one-half years. The oldest group is made up of those who came back for specific training. The mean age for this group is eighteen and one-half years.

A comparison of the reasons for returning and the year in which the decision to return was made shows that ninety per cent made up their minds to return in the twelfth grade and after graduation. This is not to be confused with the statement on page 48. That statement refers to the grade in which the curriculum that the postgraduate was then taking was decided upon. This statement refers to the time the decision to enroll as a postgraduate was made. Thus, the reasons which the postgraduates gave for returning for additional work divide themselves into two classifications—those associated with going into employment and those connected with going to institutions of higher learning.

There are several types of institutions of higher learning which attract postgraduates after they have completed their high school work.

These institutions have been classified into six groups, as shown in Table XXIII. Facts of significance are brought out in this table. The first is that only eleven per cent do not go

TABLE XXIII

DISTRIBUTION BY SEX OF 935 POSTGRADUATES ACCORDING TO PLANS FOR HIGHER
EDUCATION

PLANS FOR HIGHER EDUCATION	BOYS	GIRLS	TOTAL	PER CENT OF TOTAL
No higher education	41	67	108	11
Commercial school	29	45	74	7
Trade school	9	2	11	1
Normal school	8	32	40	4
Home economics school	0	5	5	0
Agricultural school	13	1	14	1
College or university	398	172	570	60
Other institutions	35	78	113	12
Total	533	402	935	96

on to some higher institution; and the second, that almost
sixty-one per cent go on to a college or university. The students
not going on to higher institutions plan to seek employment. The
types of institutions included under "other" are art schools, dancing schools, and other specialized schools. Seventy-four per cent
of the boys are going on to college; forty-three per cent of the
girls are going on to other types of institutions. Seven per cent
of the boys and sixteen per cent of the girls reported that they
were not continuing their education. Eleven per cent of the girls
and five per cent of the boys reported that they were going to
commercial schools.

More than half the postgraduates as a group are interested in
going to college or university. Table XXIV shows that almost
twenty-four per cent of the seniors are not going on with their
education, whereas only eleven per cent of the postgraduates are
not going on. Thus there is a larger percentage of postgraduates
than of seniors going on to colleges and universities.

A comparison of the mean intelligence quotients of the groups
planning on going on to the various higher institutions reveals
the fact that the intelligence quotients differ slightly from those
not going on. The college group has a mean quotient of one hundred seven. The mean quotient of the group not going to college
is one hundred one. The other intelligence quotients are between
these two.

TABLE XXIV

DISTRIBUTION OF 485 POSTGRADUATES AND 928 SENIORS IN THE SAME HIGH
SCHOOLS ACCORDING TO PLANS FOR HIGHER EDUCATION AND THE TYPE OF
INSTITUTION THEY PLAN TO ATTEND

PLANS FOR HIGHER EDUCATION	PER CENT OF TOTAL POSTGRADUATES PLANNING HIGHER EDUCATION	PER CENT OF SENIORS PLANNING HIGHER EDUCATION
No higher education	10	23
Commercial school	8	9
Trade school	2	1
Normal school	3	5
Home economics school	0	0
Agricultural school	2	0
College or university	54	35
Others	11	18
Not stated	6	3

The plans which the postgraduate has to attend institutions
of higher learning and the curricula or courses he took in high
school should be considered. Table XXV shows that of the stu-

TABLE XXV

COMPARISON OF 985 POSTGRADUATES ACCORDING TO COURSES FOLLOWED IN HIGH
SCHOOL AS UNDERGRADUATES AND HIGHER EDUCATION PLANS

PLANS FOR HIGHER EDUCATION	CURRICULA POSTGRADUATE ENROLLED IN AS UNDERGRADUATE								
	Gen.	Acad.	Science	Normal	Comm.	Fine Arts	Ind. Arts	H. H. Arts	Agric.
No higher education	27	31	11	3	46	6	6	3	0
Commercial school	20	21	3	4	28	4	4	0	0
Industrial school	2	6	2	0	1	1	4	0	0
Normal school	12	19	4	7	4	1	1	1	0
Home economics school	2	2	0	0	0	1	0	0	0
Agricultural school	8	3	4	0	2	0	0	0	1
College or university	119	349	95	3	59	23	28	4	3
Other	35	53	10	1	27	5	5	6	0
Total	225	484	129	18	167	41	48	14	4
Per cent in each column to college	52.8	72.1	73.65	—	35.32	56.3	58.33	29	—
Per cent in each column no further education	12.0	6.4	8.52	—	27.54	14.00	12.00	20	—

dents who were enrolled in the general course as undergraduates, fifty-two per cent of them are going to college, whereas twelve per cent are not going further in their education. A very much higher percentage of those enrolled in the academic course, or seventy-two per cent, are going on, and only six per cent end their education at the conclusion of their postgraduate work. It is especially significant that thirty-five per cent of those enrolled as undergraduates in the commercial curriculum are planning to go on to college. Twenty-seven per cent of this group are going out into employment when their work is finished. Attention is also directed to the rather high percentage of postgraduates who had been enrolled before graduation in the industrial arts course, but were planning to go to college. From all the undergraduate courses there are definite trends which appear to lead to college.

In connection with the discussion of the educational plans of the students, a fact of importance is brought out in Table XXVI.

TABLE XXVI

DISTRIBUTION BY SEX ACCORDING TO THE TIME WHEN VOCATIONAL PLANS WERE MADE BY 919 POSTGRADUATES

YEAR PLANS WERE DETERMINED	BOYS	GIRLS	TOTAL	PER CENT OF TOTAL
Before entering high school	90	93	183	20
Ninth year	38	76	114	12
Tenth year	32	28	60	6
Eleventh year	49	31	80	8
Twelfth year	82	48	130	14
Postgraduate	65	44	109	11
Plans not decided as postgraduate	149	94	243	26
Total	505	414	919	97

Twenty-six per cent of the postgraduate students have no definite plan as to what they will do when they finish their postgraduate work. The mean intelligence quotient for this group of students is one hundred six.

How many of the students received advice concerning their postgraduate course? The facts presented in Table XXVII show that forty-six per cent of the postgraduates received no advice

TABLE XXVII

DISTRIBUTION BY SEX OF 985 POSTGRADUATE STUDENTS ACCORDING TO
SOURCE OF ADVICE TO RETURN FOR POSTGRADUATE WORK

SOURCE OF ADVICE	BOYS	PER CENT OF BOYS	GIRLS	PER CENT OF GIRLS	TOTAL	PER CENT OF TOTAL
No advice	272	47	206	45	478	46
Teacher or principal	87	15	71	15	158	15
Friends	80	14	55	12	135	13
Others (family)	129	22	120	26	249	24
Total	568	98	452	98	1,020	98

concerning their postgraduate educational program. Only fifteen per cent received any guidance from the school through the teachers or other school officers.

Seventy-one per cent of four hundred two postgraduates reported that their life vocational objective was in the field of professional service. Eight per cent indicated that their vocational objective was in the field of commercial service, and nine per cent that it was in the clerical field. The percentages in the other fields of service were too small to deserve attention.

Some of the students planning to go on to college or other higher institutions are expecting to seek employment first to make sufficient money to carry them along for a time. However, most of the students included in the fifty-six per cent shown in Table XXVIII are seeking regular employment. Note that eleven per cent have definite positions in view. The thirty-seven per cent reporting favorable connections in business or industry

TABLE XXVIII

EMPLOYMENT PLANS OF THE POSTGRADUATES

PLAN	TOTAL	PER CENT OF TOTAL POSTGRADUATES
Will seek employment	557	56
Definite position in view	109	11
Have favorable connections	364	37
Will drop school work when position opens	273	27

where their relatives or friends are employed were not certain positions would be available. At least half the postgraduates seeking employment have no positions in view. In twenty-five per cent of the schools studied, as reported in the previous chapter, there are placement services available for placing these people in employment. Referring to Table XXVIII again, thirty per cent of those seeking employment will drop out of school as soon as placement is available.

When the future plans of these students who come back for additional work are considered, the question arises as to how long they plan to attend school. No particular period is outstanding, as Table XXIX shows. Thirty-seven per cent of the

TABLE XXIX

DISTRIBUTION BY SEX OF POSTGRADUATES ACCORDING TO PLANS FOR LENGTH OF STAY IN SCHOOL

LENGTH OF STAY	BOYS	PER CENT OF BOYS	GIRLS	PER CENT OF GIRLS	TOTAL	PER CENT OF TOTAL
Half semester	138	25	89	20	227	23
One semester	203	37	170	39	373	38
Two semesters	163	30	123	28	286	29
Other periods	38	7	51	11	89	9
Total	542	99	433	98	975	99

boys and thirty-nine per cent of the girls are planning to come back for one semester. Ninety per cent are not planning to spend more than one year on the work. The twenty-three per cent reporting a stay of half a semester are those who will drop out as soon as they are able to secure employment.

A study of the subjects which the postgraduate student actually takes should follow a consideration of his plans for the future.

THE SUBJECTS WHICH THE POSTGRADUATE TAKES

Since more than half the postgraduate students coming back are planning to go on to institutions of higher learning, one may expect to find the largest enrollment in the college preparatory or academic subjects. The facts are shown in Table XXX. Here it is seen that fifty-six per cent of the students are enrolled in

TABLE XXX

Subjects in Which 985 Postgraduate Students Are Enrolled

Subject Field	Boys	Per Cent of Boys	Girls	Per Cent of Girls	Total	Per Cent of Total
Academic	1,129	70	493	38	1,622	56
Commercial	327	20	706	55	1,033	36
Trade and other subjects	138	8	73	5	211	7
Total	1,594	98	1,272	98	2,866	99

academic subjects;[4] thirty-six per cent in commercial subjects;[5] and seven per cent in trade and other subjects.[6] Seventy per cent of the boys are taking academic subjects, whereas fifty-five per cent of the girls take commercial subjects. The mean number of subjects carried by each postgraduate student is two, with eighty-four per cent carrying this number.

There are some subjects which have a heavier postgraduate enrollment than others. Mathematics has the heaviest enrollment, with five times as many boys as girls in this subject. Referring to Table XXXI, it will be noted that typewriting

TABLE XXXI

Subjects Which Have the Highest Postgraduate Enrollment

Subject	Boys	Girls	Total	Per Cent of Total Number of Postgraduate Students
Mathematics	315	68	383	13
Typewriting	125	232	357	12
English	191	78	269	9
Natural science	204	59	263	9
Shorthand	43	203	246	8
Modern languages	134	83	217	7

comes next with about twice as many girls as boys. Seventy-one per cent of the students enrolled in English are boys, but in

[4] English, Ancient Languages, Modern Languages, Ancient History, European, American, or World History, Mathematics, Natural Sciences, Social Sciences, Drawing, Art, and Music.
[5] Elementary Business Training, Shorthand, Office Practice, Machine Calculation, Commercial Arithmetic, Typewriting, Bookkeeping, Salesmanship, Commercial Law, and Commercial Geography.
[6] Form Mechanics, Electricity, Carpentry, Machine Shop, Mechanical Drawing, Home Economics, Clothing Construction, Pattern Making, General Agriculture, Automobile Mechanics, Woodwork (bench), Woodwork (mill), Metal Work, Printing, Millinery, and Foods.

shorthand only seventeen per cent are boys. In modern language classes sixty-one per cent of the students are boys. In other words, the boys are in the majority in the academic subjects, whereas the girls constitute the larger part of the enrollment in the commercial subjects. Of the six subjects listed in this table, four are in the academic or college preparatory field.

Earlier in this chapter, in considering the reasons why postgraduates returned to school, it was noted that many planned to make up entrance requirements. This group includes students

TABLE XXXII

SUBJECTS WHICH HAVE THE HIGHEST NUMBER OF POSTGRADUATES REPEATING
FOR THE PURPOSE OF RAISING MARKS

ACADEMIC SUBJECT	TOTAL ENROLLED IN SUBJECT	NUMBER OF BOYS REPEATING	PER CENT OF BOYS REPEATING	NUMBER OF GIRLS REPEATING	PER CENT OF GIRLS REPEATING	TOTAL REPEATING	PER CENT OF ENROLLMENT IN SUBJECT REPEATING
English	269	95	18	24	15	119	43
Ancient language	74	29	38	8	12	37	50
Modern language	217	70	32	30	14	100	46
Ancient history	27	6	22	3	11	9	33
European, American, or world history	109	36	33	16	14	52	47
Mathematics	383	153	30	30	18	183	48
Natural science	263	93	35	22	8	115	43
Social science	100	18	18	7	7	25	25
Drawing, art, music	151	10	7	16	10	26	17

who have not taken the necessary subjects required for college entrance, those enrolled in non-academic curricula as undergraduates, and those whose marks were not high enough to warrant certification to college.

In Table XXXII are listed those subjects being repeated by the highest number of postgraduate students for the purpose of improving the mark. Note that only academic subjects are listed. Forty-two per cent of all the postgraduates enrolled in academic subjects are repeating one or more subjects, but only five per cent of the students enrolled in commercial curriculum are repeating subjects. In the trade and other subjects, fourteen per cent are repeating. That means that sixty-one per cent of the postgraduates are repeating subjects they have taken as undergraduates. Forty-eight per cent of those taking mathematics are repeating. One-half of the students taking ancient languages are repeating this subject.

It was pointed out above that the average number of subjects carried by postgraduate students is two. Many of these students carry but one subject in the academic classification, while the other or others may be either in the commercial or in the trade field. Table XXXIII shows this point. The students who are

TABLE XXXIII

REASONS FOR 985 STUDENTS TAKING POSTGRADUATE WORK AND THE SUBJECTS PREFERRED BY THE LARGER NUMBER OF POSTGRADUATES

SUBJECT	REASONS FOR TAKING POSTGRADUATE WORK								
	College in Fall	Make up Entrance Credit	Special Training	Waiting for Position	Want to Go to School Longer	Want Special Work	Advanced Credit	Not Old Enough for College	Other
Academic Total	190	237	52	114	16	77	55	41	77
English	34	47	17	25	6	11	6	8	6
Modern language	41	39	9	14	2	9	10	10	14
Mathematics	53	77	7	36	3	13	17	9	19
Natural science	34	50	6	18	3	14	15	10	20
Drawing, art	28	24	13	21	2	30	7	4	18
Commercial Total	146	43	313	246	43	76	26	40	78
Shorthand	28	7	102	58	8	21	3	11	24
Office practice	22	1	53	27	3	1	2	3	9
Typing	71	22	101	95	18	30	12	16	31
Bookkeeping	17	8	50	50	11	18	6	7	11
Commercial law	8	5	7	16	3	6	3	3	3
Trades and others Total	10	12	15	14	2	5	8	5	5
Mechanical drawing	7	10	10	8	1	5	5	3	2
Woodwork (bench)	2	0	3	4	0	0	0	0	2
Machine shop	1	2	2	2	1	0	3	2	1
Total	346	292	380	374	61	158	89	86	160

waiting until the fall to enter college distribute themselves quite evenly in all the academic and commercial subjects, with fifty-five per cent in the academic subjects and forty-two per cent in the commercial subjects. The subject with the largest enrollment in this group is typing. The students who have returned to make up college entrance requirements keep largely to the academic subjects, eighty-one per cent being enrolled in subjects in this field, whereas eighty-two per cent of those returning for special training are taking work in the commercial field. Sixty-one per cent of those returning for advanced credit are enrolled in subjects in the academic group, but sixty-five per cent of those

TABLE XXXIV

PLANS OF 985 POSTGRADUATES FOR HIGHER EDUCATION AND THE SUBJECTS IN WHICH THEY ARE ENROLLED

Subject	Not Continuing	Commercial School	Trade School	Normal School	Home Economics School	Agricultural School	College or University	Other Training	Total
Academic Total	52	29	11	35	1	17	497	79	722
English	14	7	1	10	0	2	90	16	141
Modern language	5	4	1	6	0	3	86	11	116
Mathematics	11	7	4	8	0	4	153	10	197
Natural science	9	3	3	4	0	6	106	14	145
Drawing, art	13	8	2	7	1	2	62	28	123
Commercial Total	159	123	4	21	2	2	278	136	724
Shorthand	47	37	1	4	1	0	74	44	208
Office practice	19	16	1	4	0	0	27	24	91
Typing	68	42	1	10	1	2	143	44	311
Bookkeeping	25	28	1	3	0	0	34	23	114
Trades and others Total	7	1	5	2	0	4	29	7	55
Mechanical drawing	3	1	3	1	0	2	23	3	36
Woodwork (bench)	1	0	1	1	0	1	2	3	9
Machine shop	3	0	1	0	0	1	4	1	10

waiting for positions are taking commercial subjects. It will be observed that typing receives a large percentage of students from those returning for various reasons.

By examining the subjects which the postgraduate takes and his plans for higher education, it is evident, as Table XXXIV shows, that of those not continuing seventy-three per cent take commercial subjects. Eighty-one per cent of those planning to go to commercial school are taking commercial subjects. The fact brought out in this table is that thirty-six per cent of the students planning to go to college are taking commercial subjects, principally typing, while sixty per cent are taking academic subjects. Although there are more college preparatory students taking typing than there are commercial students, it should be noted that the commercial students and those not going on distribute themselves in all the subjects in this field.

Is there any relationship between the curricula in which the postgraduate was enrolled as an undergraduate and the subjects he takes as a postgraduate? Table XXXV shows that the students in the academic and the commercial courses, as a group, were the most consistent. Seventy-three per cent of the academic

TABLE XXXV

Comparison of 985 Postgraduates According to Types of Subjects Studied and Curricula Taken as Undergraduates

Undergraduate Curricula	Per Cent of Postgraduates from Each Undergraduate Curriculum Now Taking Academic Subjects	Per Cent of Postgraduates from Each Undergraduate Curriculum Now Taking Commercial Subjects	Per Cent of Postgraduates from Each Undergraduate Curriculum Now Taking Trade and Other Subjects	Total Number of Postgraduates
General	40	51	8	511
Academic	73	15	11	802
Scientific	59	28	12	264
Normal	32	53	15	47
Commercial	21	72	6	417
Fine arts	32	60	8	123
Industrial arts	50	31	19	104
Household arts	21	74	5	43
Agriculture	28	14	28	7
Others	32	58	9	61

students remain in the academic field and seventy-two per cent of the commercial students remain in their field. The students in the general curriculum, as undergraduates, were divided almost equally between the academic and commercial fields as postgraduates. The industrial arts group left their field, with the exception of nineteen per cent of them, and went into the academic and commercial fields. There is indication here that the students in the academic or college curriculum are more certain of their vocational objective than those enrolled in the other curricula, with the exception of the commercial. Many postgraduates enrolled as undergraduates in the general, scientific, normal, industrial arts, household arts, and agriculture curricula change their vocational objectives when they reach the fifth year of high school, as indicated by the change in the subjects taken. This fact has been brought out previously in the consideration of the grade in high school when postgraduates decided on the type of course in which they were enrolled as postgraduates (page 48).

The per cent of students enrolled in the different subjects who indicated they had positions in mind, ranged from six to fifteen. For the student going on to higher institutions this is not significant, but it is significant for the student seeking permanent employment.

THE EXTRACURRICULAR ACTIVITIES OF THE POSTGRADUATE STUDENT

The extracurricular activities of the modern high school are a very real part of the educational program of the students in these schools. It is necessary, therefore, to examine these activities.

In Chapter II it was pointed out that seventy per cent of the schools either closed their extracurricular activities to postgraduates or restricted these activities. This fact is also confirmed by the information presented in Table XXXVI. Seventy-two per cent of the present postgraduate group participated in various extracurricular activities as undergraduates. The activities in which the larger number of students participated were school clubs, athletic teams, and musical organizations. When this group of students reached the status of postgraduates, thirty-three per cent engaged in extracurricular activities, i.e., thirty-nine

TABLE XXXVI

DISTRIBUTION OF 985 POSTGRADUATES AS TO GRADUATE AND UNDERGRADUATE
EXTRACURRICULAR ACTIVITIES

ACTIVITY	NUMBER OF POSTGRADUATES PARTICIPATING AS UNDERGRADUATES	NUMBER OF POSTGRADUATES PARTICIPATING AS POSTGRADUATES
Student council	98	14
Class organizations	168	18
Home room	166	57
Musical organizations	210	80
Athletic teams or squads	353	44
Dramatic or art clubs	145	38
School clubs	358	145
Fraternities or sororities	59	46
Total	1,557	442
Number not participating	276	652
Number participating	709	333
Percentage participating	72	33
Number of activities per person participating	2	1

per cent of the postgraduates who participated as undergraduates
are no longer engaged in these activities. Thus, sixty-seven
per cent of these students are not participating in extracurricular activities. The activities which attract the larger number
of students in this classification are school clubs and musical
organizations. Attention is called to the fact that although
the fraternities and sororities have the smallest representa-
tion in the undergraduate activities, they are fourth in size
on the postgraduate level. This activity lost the smallest percentage of participants when the postgraduates as a group moved
from the senior level to the postgraduate level. Not only was
there a decrease in the number of students participating in extracurricular activities, but there was also a decrease in the number
of activities which each student carried when he changed from
undergraduate to postgraduate status. As undergraduates, the
students who participated in activities of this type carried an
average of two extracurricular activities each, whereas the students who were engaging in extracurricular activities as postgraduates carried but one activity.

Thirty-seven per cent of the postgraduates were officers in their various activities as undergraduates. Only ten per cent were engaged in positions of leadership in these activities in their postgraduate year.

Sixty-seven per cent of the postgraduates are not taking any part in the extracurricular activities in the schools they are attending. When this fact is associated with the facts that sixty-six per cent of these students are not engaged in outside employment and of those so engaged the mean number of hours per week is twenty-three, and that the mean number of subjects carried by each student is two, it is evident that the larger percentage of postgraduate students are carrying on educational activities which are not in any way comparable to those carried on by the regular undergraduates in high school or in any institution of higher learning. It would appear from this evidence that at least half the time of the majority of the postgraduates is spent in undirected activity.

SUMMARY

The postgraduates studied were as selective and as high a type of students as the seniors in the same schools. Ninety-five per cent of these postgraduate students were born in the United States and seventy per cent of their fathers were born in this country. Foreign birth or parentage as a measure of selection plays little or no part in the postgraduate problem. The facts that only twenty-seven per cent of these students work in addition to going to school, that ninety-one per cent of the fathers are alive, and that sixty-six per cent of these fathers are engaged in occupations which may be classed as "the upper level" indicate that the financial problem is not a major consideration for the larger number of postgraduates. The mean intelligence quotient for the group studied is one hundred eight, practically the same as the mean intelligence quotient for nine hundred fifteen seniors from the same schools. This evidence, together with the fact that eighty-five per cent of the postgraduates were in the upper three quarters in scholastic achievement in their senior class, would show that these students as a group are equal to the seniors in the same schools in intelligence and academic achievement. The mean age for this group of students is eighteen years.

Seventy-six per cent of these students were enrolled in the academic subjects or college preparatory curricula during their senior year. Ninety per cent of the students who came back decided definitely in their senior year, or after high school graduation, to return for additional work.

The reasons why these students returned are varied but they may be grouped into four classes: namely, forty-eight per cent of the postgraduates gave reasons associated with the continuance of their education in institutions of higher learning; twenty per cent indicated that they were interested in securing specific vocational training; and sixteen per cent returned to school to keep busy until they could find employment. The remaining eighteen per cent came back for various other reasons.

It should be pointed out that in the first group there are three times as many boys as girls, whereas in the group of students returning to secure specific vocational training there are twice as many girls as boys.

Of the group going on for further educational work, sixty-one per cent are planning to enter college or university. Commercial schools will probably enroll seven per cent of the others; normal schools will carry four per cent; and the remainder will possibly be distributed among specialized schools, such as those for art, dancing, the theater, and the like.

It is significant that only fifteen per cent of the postgraduates received advice on returning to school from their high school teachers or principals. Forty-six per cent reported that they received advice from no one. With the majority of students the decision to return for postgraduate work implied that a decision had been made as to their life vocation. However, twenty-six per cent definitely reported that they were still undecided as to what their life vocational plans would be.

The employment plans of the postgraduates show that fifty-six per cent would seek employment at the conclusion of their school work. This includes some of the students who are planning to go on to college and who find it necessary to secure additional funds for this purpose. Eleven per cent had definite positions in mind.

The academic subjects are the most popular with the postgraduate student. Fifty-six per cent are enrolled in these courses, whereas thirty-six per cent are enrolled in the commercial subjects, and seven in the other subjects. The students who return to make up entrance requirements confine themselves almost entirely to the academic subjects, but the college students who do not have to give attention to this distribute their work in the academic and commercial subjects, preference being given to typing. The students who come back for specific vocational training enroll in the commercial subjects chiefly.

Forty-one per cent of the students who take academic subjects are repeating these subjects to raise their marks. In this group there are three times as many boys as girls. Practically no student enrolled in the commercial and trade curricula is repeating these subjects. Mathematics has the highest postgraduate enrollment, with forty-eight per cent of the enrollment repeating; typing, the next largest enrollment, has practically no repeaters; English, third, has forty-three per cent repeaters; natural sciences have forty-three per cent repeaters; and shorthand, no repeaters. Ancient languages have the highest per cent of repeaters, or fifty per cent.

Evidence was found to show that seventy per cent of the postgraduates who had been active as undergraduates did not participate in any of the extracurricular activities of the school. Such activity as was permitted was centered largely in school clubs and musical organizations. Fraternities and sororities showed the least decrease in membership as the students passed from undergraduate to postgraduate level.

CHAPTER IV

CONCLUSION

CHARACTERISTICS OF POSTGRADUATE STUDENTS

The postgraduates in this study come from American stock on the better economic and social level and are equal to high school seniors in the same schools in academic achievement and intelligence as measured by standardized intelligence tests. The majority of boys are interested principally in going on to college and university, while the greater number of girls are concerned with securing special vocational training in the commercial subjects. There is a group awaiting employment, a result of the present economic depression. Few have had the advice of professional educators and over half have had no counsel regarding their postgraduate educational program. Almost half the students taking academic work are repeating the subjects to raise their marks. Again, it is found that over half of them will need employment, yet only a small group have any definite positions in view. Although the average postgraduate takes just two subjects in school, only one-fourth of them are employed in addition to their school work. The greater number of these students do not participate in extracurricular activities. Thus, many postgraduate students have a large amount of undirected time. Practically all of their class work is with students younger chronologically and of different interests.

THE NEEDS OF POSTGRADUATE STUDENTS

On the basis of the characteristics of the group studied, the following are concluded to be the needs of the postgraduates:

1. *An appropriate program of extracurricular activities.* Sixty-seven per cent of the postgraduates are not participating in any of the extracurricular activities. Regardless of whether these students are going to college or into employment, they should have at least the same extracurricular opportunities as the undergraduates. However, since the postgraduates are older and have

had more experience in these activities, they will not be likely to profit much from the work if it is continued with younger students. The work should be appropriate and adapted to the level of the postgraduate student.

2. *A full program of directed activities.* It was noted that the mean number of subjects for each postgraduate was two, and that the majority of these students participated in no extracurricular activities. Furthermore, it was found that twenty-seven per cent of these students were working approximately the same number of hours per week as the senior students who were carrying at least four subjects and many of whom were participating in one or more of the extracurricular activities. The majority of postgraduates have much time which is not used in recognized directed activities. It would be wiser to insist that every postgraduate carry a complete program of studies and such extracurricular activities as he may need for his educational growth unless employed. It may be better for the postgraduate student to carry fewer subjects than four and to work on these subjects more intensively. This necessitates special assignments and checking. This program would have to be modified if the student is employed on the outside or if his health does not permit. It is to the best interest of the student that his time be taken up with worth-while directed activities.

3. *The subjects taught should be adapted to the age and experience of the postgraduate student.* This investigation shows that the students come back for academic work and for specialized vocational training. Almost half the students in the academic subjects are repeating these subjects to raise their marks in order to enter college. Postgraduate students are not only taking subjects for the first time but are also repeating subjects adapted to students who are younger and less experienced. Moreover, the possible interest which may be aroused in a subject being taken for the first time is lost to those repeating. A large number of boys are repeating English, mathematics, natural sciences, and modern languages when they were able to secure marks high enough to be certified for college in practically all their other subjects.

The postgraduates are older by a year and more experienced than the seniors in the same school; if they went directly to college, they would probably complete in six months what is ordinarily completed in a year in high school in the same subject. In college or junior college,[1] more extended texts would be used, thus better meeting the needs of these students.

Students returning for specialized vocational training are often taking work, such as typing, in classes with students in the ninth and tenth grades, when they could proceed at a much faster pace. For instance, high schools which offer commercial work on a higher level for postgraduates report that less time is required for these students to master the fundamentals than for undergraduates. Lincoln High School, Los Angeles, California, reports, "Stenography:—Time for completion of regular high school, four years; postgraduate course, five months." [2] Subjects not adapted to the age and experience of the student cannot be said to be for the best interest of the postgraduate.

4. *Advanced college credit should be granted for certain work completed.* As indicated in Chapter II, advanced college credit for postgraduate work is given by colleges and universities only under unusual circumstances. The postgraduate is only partly profiting from his school work as far as progress toward his professional objective may be concerned. If he attended a recognized junior college, his academic work would be counted and he would not lose time in moving toward his professional objective. The postgraduate is entitled to have his academic work recognized by colleges, if his mastery is equivalent to that of college standards. Examinations or inspections by colleges or state departments would determine whether the work were of a recognizable character or not.

5. *Adequate counseling service and opportunities for further exploration.* Twenty-six per cent of the students on the postgraduate level indicated that they do not know what they will do when they have completed their postgraduate work. Many of the students who were taking academic subjects reported that they were going to seek employment before going on to college. Of those seeking work, only eleven per cent had definite positions in mind. Many of these students reported as many as five changes in curricula in their undergraduate years. As one exam-

---

[1] Koos, Leonard V. *The Junior College Movement,* pp. 30 ff. Ginn and Co., 1925.
[2] Communicated to the writer, April 1931, by Rose L. Moore, Director, Postgraduate Course, Lincoln High School, Los Angeles, California.

ines the subjects which these students were taking and the reasons they gave for returning for additional work, there is evidence of inconsistencies in a large number of cases. For example, the group of students waiting for positions distributed themselves over all the academic and commercial subjects without giving much thought to securing such specific training as might make it easier for them to secure employment. Only fifteen per cent had received advice on their postgraduate program. Many of these students need further opportunity to explore and to receive guidance in this exploration in order to orient themselves vocationally.

MEETING THE NEEDS OF THE POSTGRADUATES

Are the high schools meeting the needs of the postgraduate students?

There is no evidence to show that any of the high schools studied made any provision for the extracurricular needs of these students. In a few cases some home-room activities were worked out. Twenty-six per cent of the schools reported that students of this class were eligible to participate in all the activities of the undergraduates, with the exception of interschool teams. In the case of the other schools participation was limited to certain activities or prohibited altogether.

Sixty-one schools required full-day attendance. The remaining schools practically required the postgraduate student to be present only when he was taking class work. Since the mean number of classes for a postgraduate was two, the student was present about this number of periods. Only in exceptional cases was it possible for a postgraduate to earn advanced credits for college. The only recognition given to postgraduate work by colleges was for entrance purposes.

Nine schools were offering one or two subjects, chiefly English and typing, adapted to the level of the postgraduate student. Other than this, no provision is made for meeting the curricula needs of this class of students. The work in the high schools is set up and adapted to the level of the undergraduate student. In many instances, students returning for specific vocational training were taking shorthand and typing with ninth- and tenth-grade students. Students repeating subjects to raise their marks for college entrance were going over work in classes where the younger students were meeting this subject for the first time.

Practically all schools studied had some provisions for counseling the students. As far as the postgraduate student is concerned, either this counseling is not very effective or this type of student needs more time and exploratory opportunities in which to locate and define his abilities. The latter reason is probably the more accurate statement of the case.

The larger number of high schools, therefore, are making little or no attempt to meet the needs of the postgraduate student. The reason is simple. The median number of postgraduates for the schools studied is seven. No public high school can very well afford to make special adaptations of its work for a small number of students. As brought out in this study, the only schools which have made special provisions for postgraduates have been those which had a sufficient number of students of this classification to form a class unit.

There are three ways to meet this postgraduate problem. The first is to refuse to accept postgraduate students. This is unjust to the student who needs further opportunity to prepare for higher education or to receive specific vocational training or even to explore further in educational fields.

The second way to meet this postgraduate problem is to permit the students to return and take such subjects as they need. Owing to the small number of postgraduates in the greater number of schools, it is not practicable to set up a special program. However, it is possible for these students to fit into the established school curricula and to carry a full program of worthwhile educational and extracurricular activities. It is recommended that the subjects which the student takes be enriched so as not only to command his best abilities and energies but to permit him to have this work recognized for advanced college credit or qualify him for specific vocational work. Places may be found for the postgraduate students in the extracurricular program of the school by placing them where they are not competing with younger and less experienced students but are assisting in directing intramural activities and participating in games and sports with the more mature of the undergraduate upper classmen. This system is used successfully by several high schools.

It is also possible, by means of home-room teachers or special counselors, to give these students further counsel and advice to help them to orient themselves vocationally. Thus, by enriching the subjects taken by the postgraduate, by permitting him to participate in extracurricular activities and to assist in their direction or to compete with the older undergraduate students, and by continuing counseling, it is possible for the average high school to provide a program for the postgraduate which may be worth while.

The third and most satisfactory solution to this problem, from the point of view of the postgraduate student, would be for one high school in a given area to assume the responsibility for giving an appropriate program for the postgraduate students of all the high schools in this area. The size of the area could be determined by the size and number of high schools. In some situations, it may be a definite community as in Springfield, Massachusetts; in others, it may be two or more high school districts; again, one school may be designated to handle these students for the county; or, in a large city, several schools may be selected.

The school selected to perform this function would give academic subjects on a level which would be recognized and for which credit would be given by colleges and universities as is now the situation with the better junior colleges. It would provide opportunities for exploration in professional and semi-professional fields. Adequate counseling would be given. Specific vocational training would be given appropriate to the age and experience of this student. Students would carry a full program of work and a suitable program of activities would be provided. The curricula in this school should be at least a year in length.

In this connection it should be pointed out that there is a secondary school organization already in existence in many communities of our country qualified to meet the needs of postgraduate students. This is the junior college. It is significant that in communities where there are adequate junior college facilities it was found in this study that there are practically no postgraduates enrolled in the high schools.

In communities where the junior college has been organized, the work has been set up not only to meet the needs of those going on to higher institutions, but also to provide for those students who need specific vocational training and who receive no further formal training.

Evidence has been presented to show that in many high schools postgraduates are not encouraged to return. The writer feels that if provision were made for these students, as suggested above, many high school graduates not now in school would return. This has been the experience of the schools cited in this study where an attempt has been made to provide a suitable program for these students. It is not a question of encouragement but rather one of providing appropriate opportunities.